CLASSIFIED

Love

CLASSIFIED

Love

A Guide to the PERSONALS

SHERRI FOXMAN

McGRAW-HILL BOOK COMPANY

New York   St. Louis   San Francisco   Bogotá   Guatemala
Hamburg   Lisbon   Madrid   Mexico   Montreal   Panama
Paris   San Juan   São Paulo   Tokyo   Toronto

1 2 3 4 5 6 7 8 9 0 F G R F G R 8 7 6 5 4 3 2

ISBN 0-07-021756-4

LIBRARY OF CONGRESS CATALOGING IN PUBLICATION DATA
Foxman, Sherri.
Classified love.
1. Personals.   I. Title.
PN4839.F6   070.4′44   82-59
ISBN 0-07-021756-4 (pbk.)   AACR2

Book design by Christine Aulicino.

TO

Herbert J. Weiss (doctorate professional) for helping author (electorate professional) to transfer his belief in her to the pages of this book . . .

ACKNOWLEDGMENTS

For putting up with me all these years I thank my father, Howard Foxman (I'll buy my own car from now on!), and for putting up with me for a few of these years I thank my stepmother, Ketty.

For being the best grandmother in the whole wide world I thank Grandma Julie, and for taking care of me to the best of anyone's ability I thank Rosa M. Phillips (aka Rosie).

For help while under the line of fire I thank Jean Carothers, Tema Greenberger, Karen Rhea, Sandy Shovary, and Denise Szczepanski.

For intermittent bouts of patience and support, thanks to Carl LoPresti.

And most of all for unending encouragement, support, and a good ear, I thank my friends—Diane Hanowitz; Marty and Lynn Helstein and the B; Larry Gogolick; Marty Davis; Eileen Levy; the Saltzmans—Michael, Fran, Sydney, Shibbie, Gigi, and Barb; the Toth sisters—Sandy and Barb (Daly); the Toth parents; Paul Daly; ChiChi; Joan Azen; Towney and Jane Coleman; Margaret and Paul Zusky; David Creps; Patti Morse Marks and her brother, Kenny; Margo Luntz; Hugh and Tom Leider; the Markses; the Unions; Mer and Jules Altshuler; Nick LaJoe and Margo; Ruth and Alan Jaffe; the LoPrestis—Fran, Joe, Mary Jo, Gus and Kristyn; Sharon Grossman and Pat Crago; Al Grimm; Ray DiNallo; Jan Rubins; Sheldon Jacobs; Bruce Schwartz; Pinkie, Charlie, and

Doc; and my not often seen friends Barbara Hirsch, Walter Smith, and Mary Boyle.

A special thought to Tracy Williamson.

Unmentionable thoughts to Don Green.

A large amount of gratitude mixed with a great deal of thanks for Larry Pesses.

And for unbelievable patience, support, loyalty, and more than the usual sibling involvement a sincere thanks to my best friend and brother, Steve.

CONTENTS

INTRODUCTION

YOU HAVE ONE MINUTE to convince this 30-year-old female that you are the one! I park in fire lanes; I shop where there's no line; I sit in the first row at concerts; I'm most comfortable in cords; I'm superintelligent but not an intellectual. I don't mind wine but love is the drug I'm interested in. Aggressive, silly, frightened and lonely—one from whom you never know what to expect seeks same—to share ups and downs, sillies and nons—a man who is independent and doesn't need me to entertain him. Call for a chance to meet a most interesting and unusual woman . . . 555-1404.

A practical joke? A come-on? Not at all. This is a real ad I placed in the classified section of a local magazine. Before the magazine was even on the stands or in the mail, I received a call from the typesetter who had set the ad for publication. My answering machine hadn't even been connected when my newly installed

xiv   INTRODUCTION

unlisted phone rang. Knowing it had to be a wrong number, you can imagine my surprise when I was greeted with, "Hi, Sweetcakes, how ya doing? Great ad!" Within a month thousands of Cleveland-area men found their way to the telephone to bare their souls in an effort to get a date with this mystery woman:

I say, let me make a 60-second response so that I may help procure your mysterious presence. . . . Let me put it this way: I'm 32 years old, single 6 feet tall, change my clothes in a telephone booth and leap tall buildings in a single bound . . . 555-3848.

Sorry you didn't answer this, dear. . . . This is Robert Redford, and I don't make second calls. . . .

Depending on what your exact demands and specifications are, I could be exactly what you're looking for. If you want to have fun, and make tax-free money, call me at 555-4312.

The phone was still ringing nine months later. The ad generated so much interest that a local television personality asked me to star on his daily talk show; he then played my answer tape on the air after sharing the ad with the audience. I received calls from newspaper reporters begging for interviews, and from women pleading for some of the names and phone numbers, offering to pay a commission.

But this ad appeared after I had some experience with classified love. My first attempts did not cause such a sensation. Those early ads were sincere but boring; average response, 25. With experience I became more original and as a result I received more responses and a better cross-section of respondents. During the past two years I placed a dozen ads for myself and received several thousand responses. I dated some of the respondents, but so far I haven't found Mr. Right. I'm still looking, and still placing ads.

When my friends learned of my success with the personals, they asked me to help them create ads for themselves. This allowed me to give full rein to my creativity:

> FEMALE (41) Italian, seeks male of same descent for traditional maid-oriented relationship. Do not answer this ad unless you are a confirmed chauvinist, like to be waited on and have never cleared the table.

The responses grew.

My adventurous friends wanted more suggestive ads, so I wrote:

> WOMAN (27), seeks roommate to share bed and board. One bed, one bored.

Things got out of hand.

Then I approached the unapproachable:

> MARRIED WOMAN (early 30s) looking for discreet playmate (attached or un) for adventurous romping and total fulfillment. NO STRINGS.

All hell broke loose.

And so . . . Authoress, early 30s, wishes to uncover all sides of this controversial approach to romance and sex and tell all to the millions of dedicated Americans who daily read the personals and wonder, "Who would do something like this?"

CLASSIFIED

Love

1.

GET PERSONAL

THE PARTICIPATORS

What type of person pursues classified love? You name it! From doctors to sex fiends, from prison inmates to businessmen, from clergy to perverts, you'll find them all in the personals.

WHO ADVERTISES

POETS:

DAMN, this sounds so trite. Should I say I'm bright? I'm a special man but try as I might, there's no other way. You'll just have to write.

DOCTORS:

SINGLE WHITE FEMALE PHYSICIAN—50 (from a Protestant, professional family background), nondrinker, nonsmoker, 5'8", blond, blue-eyed, very

1

healthy, intelligent, attractive, and vivacious, looks and acts younger than her age. Likes good conversation and laughter on a one-to-one basis or in a small congenial group. Interested in people. Prefers reading to TV. Loves classical music. Enjoys nature walks and swimming. Seeks widowed or divorced man, approximately aged 45 to 55, in good health, who is interested in developing a friendship which might lead to marriage. Qualities sought are: well-above average intelligence and education, integrity, sincerity, loyalty, warmth, kindness, a good disposition, and a sense of humor. Would like someone who does not smoke cigarettes and who is either a very light drinker or a nondrinker. Would especially like to meet someone in a "people-oriented" profession, such as medicine, psychology, law, social worker, teaching; or in a "word-oriented" profession, such as writing or editing.

DENTISTS:

ATTRACTIVE MALE DENTIST, 29, 5'9", Jewish, dominant personality, but easy to get along with, seeks basically docile female for ongoing or permanent relationship. Prefer 'almost' heavyset women and those who know what they want.

CLERGY:

SWF—27, clergywoman, 5'8", attractive, warm, funny, sensitive, educated, vibrant, eclectic interests, romantic, vulnerable, and very human, seeks sensitive, liberated SWM, who desires open and honest communication in a committed relationship; one to talk with, laugh with, cry with, and play with.

MARRIEDS:

WELL-TO-DO professional man, 5'10", 135 pounds, would like to meet intelligent, beautiful woman, 21–40, of artistic inclinations and not averse to mistresshood.

PILOTS:

COMMERCIAL PILOT living on island of Aruba 7mon States 5mon into flying scuba sailing travel seeks SF 29–37 adventuresome to share permanent relationship.

SAILORS:

FEMALE SAILING CREW for 26' cruising/racing boat sought by middle-aged professional man.

INMATES:

LONELY? I am. I'm incarcerated right now and in need of someone who would enjoy sharing feelings and thoughts about any and everything through correspondence, and visits if possible. I'm black, but color me lonely, 25, understanding, and sincere.

FATTIES:

WOMAN, 35, sense of humor, intelligent, affectionate, desires man with the same sterling qualities who can appreciate the virtues of a large woman.

FETISHISTS:

BALLOONS ANYONE? Pop a balloon and turn me on! Bright, successful, attractive guy wonders if anyone shares his uncommon fetish. Write.

WHO RESPONDS

I received answers from doctors, lawyers, executives from major companies, bankers, entertainers (some local and some who claimed to be staying in our city while making a film), airline pilots who are in our city one night a week, and self-made businessmen. I even received a response from a minister and one from a self-confessed gigolo. I was amazed by the number of responses I received, but I was more amazed by the content of the letters and, sometimes, the items that were enclosed.

Some people enclosed their business cards. They tended to be lawyers, business owners, and executives with impressive titles.

This is one way for a person to tell about himself without having to write too much, relying on the fact that his title or the fact that he owns his own business will encourage you to contact him. Another possibility is that it lends credibility to his response. Someone who sends his card is not going to try anything shady, especially since you (and your family and friends) know who he is and where to find him.

Some of the business cards that were enclosed had messages written on the backs; these obviously were very short (not too much will fit on a 2″ × 3½″ card).

Please call me. I want a date . . .

Others sent the business card but didn't bother to write anything. And then others sent the business card attached to a short note or even a lengthy letter that explained a little more about themselves and asked me to call. The following is from a vice-president of a major corporation:

*If you are interested in becoming acquainted,
please call my private line—use the name Mary
Win to get past my secretary.*

One man even sent his business card, a lengthy letter, and a tearsheet from *Who's Who* with his name circled.

I purposely did not request a photo in any of my personals ads; it might inhibit people. I assumed people would not send their photo to an ad in a magazine. I was wrong.

Some people enclosed photos of themselves in birthday suits, in bathing suits, even in bathing suits and socks. A lot of men displayed their cars. One was especially interesting—a man proclaimed as he stood in front of an obviously expensive sports car:

*The beard is gone, so is the car; all that remains is
an attractive gentleman . . .*

Some people sent two pictures—different poses (right and left side). None sent front and back. One man even enclosed a postcard with his picture on the front, and on the back the phrase

What do you think?

being the whole of his letter. He's got confidence.

Some respondents just sent a picture with a note on the back to call them. Models sent pictures ripped out of magazines with their faces circled. I also received several newspaper clippings and articles with the writer's picture featured (or so it was claimed). All in all, passport photos were the most popular.

I was surprised by how many people enclosed a self-addressed stamped or unstamped envelope. I haven't figured out why some were stamped and some were not, except for this man's letter:

> *When you answer this letter, I'll send you a stamp to pay you back for the postage. I would include a s.a.s.e. but if you don't answer, why waste 15¢?*

The people who sent newspaper clippings about themselves were usually celebrity types: racing car drivers, sports personalities, etc. One man sent an article claiming he was worth billions. The photo in the article was obviously pasted on with his name typed below it and then photostated.

Many people sent company promotional items such as news releases and advertising inserts. These usually included a blurb stating a description of their job, length of time with the company, title—all mostly accompanied by a photograph.

Men who sent a Xeroxed form letter had probably answered every female within a two-hundred-mile radius of their home. Here is an example:

> *Dear Friend: Do you like fun . . . excitement? Would you like a sensuous, playful companion? Would you like intellectual stimulation? Would you like a caring, understanding friend? If so, YOU would like meeting me . . . I am a very successful international attorney, published author, lecturer, financial and tax consultant. I'd also like a traveling companion. . . . Have lots of worldwide travel coming up for clients.* **I'll be living in your city and other cities sometime soon.**

And another letter, again photostated, came with a newspaper article describing the individual:

My dear lady: I presume you to be a delightful person. . . . I trust you will appreciate this evaluation. Why don't you stop by for cocktails one afternoon (bring a lady friend if you wish) . . . by appointment only . . . to my fabulous ¼ of a million dollar executive suite? I am a world traveler many times over. I have been everywhere and have seen everything twice. . . . A million-dollar gentleman with a good sense of humor who doesn't smoke, drink, gamble, or meet women in bars . . .

Some men never give up. I received, for example, seven cards and letters, mostly greeting cards, from one person in answer to one ad:

June 30:

Saw your ad . . . and have been in a state of excitement ever since as I find older women tantalizing, as was your ad. Accordingly, I would like to meet you perhaps for a relationship characterized by socialization, syncopation, sensualization, and sexualization. How about getting together for lunch on the 10th at 12:30 PM? I'll plan to meet you in the bar and will be wearing a blue blazer with tie. If not, call the bar and ask for me (Jack). P.S. I'm planning on bringing my bathing suit . . . I believe they have an indoor pool with outdoor sundeck . . . please keep this idea in mind.

July 1:

I hope by now you received my letter dated June 30. I hope we can get together on the 10th but if not and if time permits write me to arrange another meeting.

July 2:

On third thought, perhaps you should write to confirm our meeting . . . perhaps as a result of my first two notes to you, you either would not like to meet me or you would like to meet on another day at another location . . . however, the 10th is best for me.

July 7:

Something has come up and consequently I may not be able to meet you to make our unconfirmed luncheon date this Thursday. If at all possible, I'll meet you at the prearranged location; if not, perhaps we can reschedule. . . . Please write me and tell me what length of time it takes for one of my notes to be forwarded to you . . . I need to know the lead time to arrange a date.

July 11:

Enclosed matchbook cover from restaurant/ inn. . . . Looked for you yesterday but apparently you weren't around . . . if I don't hear from you within two weeks, I'll assume you weren't serious.

July 19: Sent greeting card about "why don't you write??"

Please write me.

July 30: Sent another greeting card

I'd still like to meet you . . . please write and confirm receipt of my previous notes, cards, and letters.

Then there was the man who responded to both a "MARRIED WOMAN (early 30s)" and a "PROSPER-OUS FEMALE (50ish)" with the same letter, changing only the age:

*Having read your ad nearly two hours ago, I must mention, yes, I'm fully aroused! I am very firm and trim . . . and your ad was encouragingly arousing . . . your age is perfect! In fact, a woman in your age bracket **early 30s** excites me to the fullest. The reason for this I surmise is what happened to me when I was about 14. It involved a seductive **33 year old** neighbor whose lawn I used to mow. If you'd like, I'll tell you about it sometime. In any case, because of her, I've developed an affinity, yes, an ardent desire for a woman in your age bracket. **I'm not far behind myself.** My mind envisions you to be a passionate, eager, seductive, and responsive woman . . . full of flame, and kindled with passion, overflowing.*

*Having read your ad nearly two hours ago, I must mention, yes, I'm fully aroused! I am very firm and trim . . . and your ad was encouragingly arousing . . . your age is perfect! In fact, a woman in your age bracket **early 50s** excites me to the fullest. The reason for this I surmise is what happened to me when I was about 14. It involved a seductive **55 year old** neighbor whose lawn I used to mow. If you'd like, I'll tell you about it sometime. In any case, because of her, I've developed an affinity, yes, an ardent desire for a woman in your age bracket. My mind envisions you to be a passionate, eager, seductive, and re-*

sponsive woman . . . full of flame, and kindled with passion, overflowing.

This man answered a Married Woman seeking diversion and also a woman looking for a Sugar Daddy, except to "MARRIED WOMAN" he wrote as a woman. It was obviously the same handwriting and the dates on the letters are the same.

> *Sorry I'm late in answering your ad, but if you're still interested in meeting a nice person for adventurous romping, I wish you would give me a call at 555-4422. My name is Cindy and my boyfriend's name is Ed. If he answers, it's o.k. too. He's very understanding and enjoys me and him having a good time. We are both very open about everything. I am 5'8", blond, 120, and take a size 8–9. My measurements are 36-23-36. Ed is 6'3", brown hair, 190, and in very good shape. He is 39 and I'm 24. We both would like to meet you. Maybe you would like either Ed or myself or even both.*
>
> > *Cindy*

> *Sorry I'm late in getting a letter off to you, but time just flies by. I saw your ad some time ago, and if you're still interested in what your ad said, I would like to hear from you. I attend a lot of out-of-town meetings, dinners and would like someone to attend them with me. I travel from coast to coast and sometimes out of the country. So if you have no ties and can get away, I would be more than happy to make it worth your while. I am 43 [note the age], tall, in good shape, and enjoy going out to dinner and shows, so if you are interested call me at 555-4422.*
>
> > *Ed*

Finally, some people decide that if they're going to answer one ad, they might as well answer them all. Note the different ways the same man responded at various times to different ads:

A SUPERIOR FEMALE:

Greetings—call me . . . let's see if I meet your qualifications!

A CATHOLIC FEMALE:

It's certainly nice to hear that there's someone who cares about religion and the other finer things of life. Call me . . . let's talk.

A MISTRESS:

Save me from my terrible handwriting . . . call me at 555-3236 evenings around 6:30. Talk to you then!

A DIVORCED WOMAN:

Hi! My name is Jack—I'm 30 years old and a professional career man . . . divorced, no children . . . ready and willing to meet a super girl who feels life is great! Let's talk.

I heard from unbelievably honest married men

I am married—not happily and live in one city and work in another. I spend two or three nights in local hotels and lately it has just become a little bit lonely. I find myself unable to make the bar scene maybe because of shyness, too long married, afraid of involvement, or a combination of all three. I'm assuming your ad is on the level and you are a reasonably attractive woman.

Although married my relationship has been ice for the last ten years with no improvement in the foreseeable future. . . . I enjoy sex with no holds barred, satisfaction for both being paramount.

I would like very much to meet you. I'll be honest with you from the start. I'm happily married and probably can't change that.

Men with physical attributes

*In looks, I am probably not everybody's dreamboat, but **I'm no Quasimodo** either.*

*You should have some sort of biography on me. Married, 5'9", 160 lbs., absolutely **outrageously good looking,** work out at Vic Tanney's, have small boat, work as a plumber, into a little jogging, especially in the evenings when I can run nude on a high school track. I am a good listener with a body that doesn't want to quit.*

*As for the vital statistics, I have a summer tan and **sexy legs.***

*I am a male with brown hair, brown eyes, and stand 5'4" in no shoes and weigh about 120 lbs., but **I am not skinny.***

*I am a white male, 5'10" and clean. While I have a large ego, I feel odd giving a verbal description. . . . I am an attorney and sexually active, **well hung** and with great stamina.*

*Vital stats: (1) early thirties, (2) white, (3) 5'7", (4) 170 lbs., (5) **good teeth and hair (full head),** (6) dimples, (7) available at your leisure.*

*I'm a practicing podiatrist . . . I am married . . .
I am interested in more than a humdrum life. I do
not want to appear egotistical, but I have been
told **I am above average in looks and masculinity.***

*I better tell you what I look like. I'm 5'10", 185
lbs., with brown curly hair and blue eyes. I've
been told by women that **I have a very nice ass**
. . . I am an exceptionally good lover.*

*If you're good looking, medium to slender and
want to live out what other people dream about,
then we should not waste time. If you are a body
lover, I'm 6'0" tall, 175 lbs., **trim and built.** Like I
said, even if you've had a lot of responses already, remember all of us guys aren't alike and
variety is the spice of life.*

Men from out of town

*I'm here from Hollywood, California filming in
Cleveland until the end of August. Please call.*

*I am a business consultant and travel from New
York to Washington monthly. My next trip will be
December 10th and 11th.*

*I am a 37-year-old fellow with a two-bedroom flat
in Brooklyn. Perhaps if you ever come to New
York City, after all there's only Pennsylvania between us, you could stay at my place for a week,
or perhaps a weekend for some fun. . . . Money
is no object and I could come visit you in Ohio.*

*Could you use a pen pal who maybe three times
per year might actually materialize in the flesh in
your city?*

Men with money

I'm seeking a relationship with an intellectual young woman who wishes to share a new experience. . . . I am self-employed and reside on my yacht. . . . I would like an opportunity to share an evening with you over cocktails, dinner, and a warm fire.

I'm a nice-looking young man, tall, strong, and very intelligent and above all very very rich.

Your ad looks most interesting. I'm recently divorced, no children, no debts, and I own my own large home. . . . I just had a complete physical and am in A-1 condition, no diseases, no history of cancer, brain tumors, no heart problems, no genetic disturbances. My annual income is above $25,000 per year and getting better all the time.

I am a very successful 41-year-old self-made millionaire who is married and college educated and own several million dollars of real estate around this area. This statement is not made of course because I am conceited but rather careful.

Men who fit no category

I'm a man which has power and greatness, which I feel is indestructible because it is built not on fear, envy and suspicion . . . nor is it won at the expense of others but founded on hope, trust and friendship . . . all I ask is that you be individually independent of yourself; that you be able to stand for yourself and be strong . . . the purpose of writing is to enforce the sense we have of the future and to enforce the sense we have of responsibility —of understanding our roles in the shaping of a good relationship —experience is development and development is destruction . . . a fall in the pit is a gain of wit. . . . May the Universal Powers Bless & Protect you forever!

That I am writing this letter in reference to reading about you, that I would want to meet? That is, if perhaps me being a black guy does not turn you off? To decide upon discernment and related lifestyles and referring fornication nature to discuss. Therefore, subjects of personal interests appear not to hesitate due to these sensuous ways of looking at what's happening to us —responsive however about making the kinda peace. Hopefully that all goes well for a safe and secure form of discretion goals of romance for having fine feelings to share. I am of 3/21/30. Having the right kind of nature for people of different skin color, I am tall and about 185 manly pounds of good sensuous humor —who hope that I can stimulate enough to drop back in on me, all due to what's happening to us . . . writing does appear to bring out the very best, to share in interest for the other —

I noticed your ad in the August 80 magazine. I noted that you are attractive, outgoing, and interested in meeting men. It seems to me that you would like gifts from these men in exchange for your favors. The problem with this situation, however, is that these gifts are not given regularly.

I have an alternative to offer you. I run a legitimate escort service, which is listed in the yellow pages under "ESCORT SERVICES" . . . 10% finder's fee paid for referrals.

On a whim and with great curiosity, I decided to answer your article. . . . I offer the following info on myself . . . free, white, 33, 5'11", have good white-collar job . . . interests include tennis, softball, bullshitting. . . . Things I am not— fanatic, blowhard, drunk, macho man, kidnapper, addicted to any drug, clone, schizo, under warranty, dull, flaky, public nuisance, or left-handed. . . . Things I am—intelligent, articulate, a dreamer, a storyteller, financially astute. . . . I've never done this before, it's kind of kinky . . . still, if I don't hear from you, let me at least wish you well and compliment you on your courage for running the ad.

Men you wouldn't want to meet

I have a minimal amount of time to sift thru the crap at singles bars. . . . I am looking for an attractive, no bullshit, upfront companion to show off in public.

I was contemplating being an escort; however, I'm so choosy about the company I keep that if a woman is not intelligent, sophisticated, and attractive (with a warm heart) no amount of money or gifts could buy my time.

I hate to write, so I hope you take it as a compliment that I'm answering your ad . . . considering this, why don't you call me?

I have a charm about me which people consider rare. My appearance is striking. So as you can well imagine, I'm very good-looking. It doesn't stop there. I am an intelligent, common sense person who believes in justice.

Call only if your friends or people you know refer to you as lovely, classy, good-looking and really well built. If you have these qualities or think you do, call, otherwise, throw this away.

I am a lawyer. . . . I'm successful which means I have a drive that pushes me to succeed. That drive extends to other facets of the personality that need fulfillment also. My doctor says I have an unusually strong drive. I handle it well. I'm so satisfied with myself that I seek satisfaction in bringing satisfaction. I cannot remember a complaint. . . . I'm not an egotist, just know where I'm at and I know I'm fascinating company.

Please send a recent photo, your telephone number, and 20 ¢. Warmly, Gene.

First, I don't think a magazine ad is a really nice way to meet people. I am not sure why I put my ad in this magazine in the first place. If I have to do it again, I will never use any magazine to meet people. Mostly one meets losers and I meet a lot of girls who replied to my ad, and all but one are in this group. I would never advise any of my friends to use the magazines for this purpose. We moved in this area around August and someone mentioned about the magazine to me. I had a mistress for about a year when I was in Toledo, but when I moved in this area I started to look for a playmate. I mentioned playmate and a few other intimate words in my original ad that I submitted to this magazine, but apparently they told me they would have to edit my ad to take a few words out. I replied to them to go ahead and change it any way they saw fit, and what you read is the final version of that editing they decided. One thing I can tell you is that I'm far more qualified than you are and probably can make better ads than you can. I just wish they would have left my original ad in without changing to meet their publishing needs. The type of experience I had with the girls who answered my ad tells me I don't have to convince anyone about me. The girls have to do that to me. If you are interested in the type of relationship I mentioned, tell me something about you and send your photo and a phone number where I can reach you.

My favorites
A penpal:

> *I am incarcerated but I desire to **engage in sensually provocative correspondence,** to share in your desires and to share mine . . . hope you enjoy full arousal.*

A strange person:

> *Am interested in rapping with you. Call or write and be discreet. If you don't call, would like to have **revealing photo anyway.***

A humorist:

> *I am very picky about food, sometimes petty, too sensitive, possessive, slightly materialistic, and sort of manic-depressive. **But who's perfect?***

A politician:

> *I am responding with great desire . . . I believe you are a dream come true. . . . I'm educated and worldly, refined and **republican**.*

A good sport:

> *I do not perform the act of writing to personals, but your ad, being well worded and 'catchy' has motivated me to give it **the proverbial "college try."***

An enterprising individual:

> *If you have too many replies for your 'playmate,' please **pass my name along to one of your attractive girlfriends**.*

WHY THEY RESPONDED

> *I know it can be very difficult meeting someone that a person can relate to. At times the opportunity isn't all that great. **It's possible this may be as good a way as any**.*

> *I'm considered a striking green-eyed blonde, a very young 37, single for two years, with a neat 6-year-old son. Very sociable but **dislike the bar scene**.*

> *I had noticed your ad in this month's magazine and after I had read the article about personal ads it dawned on me **I'm not the only one looking for a heart to beat together with**.*

> *So what the heck. After reading the article in the current issue of our magazine, I figure **it might be fun** to write so here goes.*

*Attorney 'never married' largely matching your check list —**wants to take a chance.***

*I come to your city four times a year, but my company is considering transferring me on a permanent basis and therefore **a good place for me to meet someone is through advertising.** Someone said that women have a difficult time meeting men but with the ratio being what it is I feel men have difficulty meeting women.*

*Have recently moved here and found it **difficult to meet someone sincere and make friends.***

Some weren't sure

***I'm as unaccustomed to answering classified ads as you are to placing them** so forgive me if my response doesn't follow the prescribed form, if there is one.*

***You took a chance by placing the ad —I'm taking one by answering** but at this point you're ahead —you have a name and a telephone number.*

*You know what you want and apparently are ready to take risks. . . . **How do you tell the weirdos from the sincere?***

*Saw your ad quite a few months ago, and **it took this long for me to get the nerve**. . . . I fear going into singles bars as I feel like 'meat on the hook.'*

Some had fantasies

Dear Marie: Happy summer! That's probably not your name but I happen to like it.

Read carefully with an open mind of two sincere young men also in their thirties, who desire to fulfill any and all of your wildest fantasies. We are both unattached—tall—and assure you good-looking. We await your reply to set up a pleasure-ful meeting at a mutual place and time of convenience. Please respond. To Rich and David . . . willingly yours.

To satiate your every desire and any way you desire would be my one consuming passion. . . . Your expression of full enjoyment would be satisfaction enough for me. To receive more would be icing on the cake. If it's thorough lovemaking you're seeking then I'm sure I can be as good as you wish and invoke in me. You sound like the answer to my wildest dreams so luscious, provocating, tantalizing, gorgeous hunk of pulchritude and your every wish will be my command. I am not expecting or demanding a pretty woman.

General appearance: Cute for a short guy (this is according to my wife and past girl friends). Oh yes, I am married. . . . Fantasy: to have a tall wealthy lady dressed in a black evening gown abduct me to her sailing yacht; sail me away to an unknown destination; slowly and seductively undress first herself and then me, as I lay helplessly watching. As the tropic ocean breeze covers our bodies, she wraps her long thin legs around me and we make love so successfully that we do not even notice the boat sinking in the warm ocean water drowning the two of us. Beliefs: that both men and women should wear sexy underwear. Reason for answering ad: I have never made love to a lady older than myself. The idea sounds excit-ing and it sure would be nice to have someone to talk to.

Others were looking for discreet 007 arrangements

If you would like to meet I'd be glad to meet you at the Pat Joyce Tavern. If this is unacceptable, please place an ad in the personal section of the newspaper. I'll be there from 1:30 to 2:30 Tues-day, July 1st, wearing a light beige suit.

On July 1, 1980, I'll be enjoying lunch at the Mar-riott at 11:52 AM. Please join me—wear a smile—let's plan our escape.

If you wish to pursue, please call my watering hole lunchtime only on Friday, 12:00 to 12:30, and ask for Jack.

If you're interested, let's meet for a drink. You choose the day at 12:00 noon sharp. Put the fol-lowing ad in the business and personal section of the newspaper: 'Attention Tom, let's meet on day of week and date.' Run it three days. That day at the bar ask for Tom.

. . . Let's meet in the lobby of the Holiday Inn between 6:00 and 6:30 on July 30th. . . . Carry a small book or flower so I can recognize you.

Call and ask for Mr. Smith and say you need some plumbing done. I'll get on the phone and you give me a place and time to meet you or call you. Don't pay any attention to what I say because I'll be doing some doubletalk while actually listening. Please call. I need to meet you. If my wife answers, don't hang up.

If you'll be good enough to phone me at a specific time, I'd make sure to be there and free to speak. . . . It sounds so cloak and dagger trying to be discreet. Let's try it. How about 11:30 Tuesday and/or Thursday—if nothing else, I'll learn if you are punctual.

There were those men who felt convincing me of their sexual eagerness and prowess, or just discussing sex suggestively, would assure my contacting them.

I'm 28, slim, good-looking, and submissive.

I've never found a woman who is reasonably responsive that I couldn't more than satisfy and this is no idle boast. I get more complaints about lack of sleep than I do lack of performance. I decided while I was still a virgin that I would not be satisfied if my partner wasn't satisfied first.

No B.S. I'm intelligent, congenial, witty, attractive, clean, and discreet (like everyone else who responds to your ad). I would suggest a matinee at an Art Theatre for our first date.

I love giving and receiving _____. You fill in the blank.

I'm not looking for someone to make a quick trip to the bedroom with.

I love to have sexual experiences; straight, french, or any other exotic way that would bring you pleasure . . . by the way, my mailing name below is not my real name.

White male, 32, warm, affectionate, and super in bed, happily married but looking for some extra play. . . . I have flexible hours, I'm quiet, soft spoken but strictly good time. Give it a shot.

Your ad was interesting to read, give me a call, 69 is my number and 69 is my game . . . call me at the above number between 0800 to 1500 hours during the week.

I have an athletic build (6' and 190 lbs.) and like to enjoy life. During my college days I earned the nickname of "big Ern" and I would love to show you just how I got that name . . . perhaps we could get together and enjoy some sex-filled summer days. Signed Big Ern.

I'm not bragging or saying I'm anything great, but I think I'm somewhat of a different breed when it comes to sexual relations. . . . My sexual needs come second. . . . I am totally uninhibited, I'll do anything to satisfy the woman, leaving nothing to the imagination. . . . I am also very healthy sexually, and have a very strong sex drive.

I enjoy all forms of romantic lovemaking with the emphasis of being gentle and assuming total fulfillment and satisfaction from our partner first before any mutual fulfillment is reached. I'm very open minded and willing to try any fantasy you may desire. I'm experienced enough so that we can be very comfortable. . . . I recently took some very candid Polaroid pictures but I'll save those if and when you may be interested.

2.

PERSONAL PURSUIT

SINCERELY YOURS

STEPPED-ON GIRL (30), bright, witty, and special, looking for sincere relationship. *Please*, no vegetables.

I was having dinner at a friend's house and was
telling him that I was thinking of placing a personal ad
in our city magazine but that I didn't know how to
describe myself. I had just gotten over my latest (well,
almost) and was feeling pretty low. Before I knew it, my
host had written an ad that he felt described me per-
fectly (at least that evening). I must admit, he did a
pretty decent job—I certainly felt stepped-on, and I
hadn't eaten my vegetables.

On a whim, I decided to run the ad and see what
would happen. I received a fairly good response—
seventy-one letters (the average response to an ad was
twenty to twenty-five). Most of the responses were

painstakingly boring, but there were those few who could relate:

> *I am a special man who has been folded and spin-dled much too often.*

> *Saw your ad and couldn't resist answering as I also have a size 7½ stamped in the middle of my back.*

> *Sorry to hear you've been stepped on but I bear a few scars myself . . . not to change the subject, but do green beans and carrots really answer these ads?*

Because of this woman's sorry state, most of the men felt a need to be warm, friendly, and overwhelmingly sincere, but some couldn't avoid showing their true colors:

> *I hate to write; take it as a compliment that I'm even answering. Considering this, why don't you call me?*

> *Someone special should be attractive and not fat.*

Then there were the guys who just didn't have much confidence in their looks. I'm not surprised that they answered a stepped-on girl . . .

> *I am somewhat of an entertainer . . . I'm admittedly overweight (200–233 glutenate).*

> *I am 5'10" tall, on the heavy side, and below average in appearance.*

and some who were confused about their appearance altogether . . .

I'm 37, 5'8" to 5'10" tall, 150–160 lbs., with light brown hair and green or blue eyes.

I am 6 inches tall, 170 lbs., possibly, reasonably attractive looking.

and let's not forget those understanding individuals one never meets in real life . . .

I was attracted to your ad because you were honest enough to admit an occurrence of a traumatic relationship. . . . Meat and Potatoely Yours.

There isn't a soul in this world that hasn't been stepped on once or twice . . . it isn't the end of the world, you know!

*I am sorry that some guy hurt you but, keep in mind, **we're not all that bad!***

In conclusion: if you're stepped-on, keep it to yourself.

HI! WHAT'S YOUR SIGN?

PISCES/ARIES woman (30s), born on cusp—more ram than fish—seeks compatible partner for charting future plans. Astrologically speaking, of course, you'll thank your lucky stars. NO VIRGOS.

We are past the Age of Aquarius, so to speak. Not too long ago, every time you stepped into a bar you were approached by a perfect stranger saying, "Hi! What's your sign?"

If you are like me, you yawned, stretched, and spilled your drink, or just walked away. However, some were really into astrology and still are. Using myself as a guinea pig, I wrote an ad to appeal to those who are still daily horoscope readers. Interestingly enough, the respondents were mostly professional.

Many people who answered the ad ignored its astrological basis; others ingeniously made up for their lack of knowledge (or lack of understanding). For example, one man answered this ad and different ads placed by thirty of my friends, with the same letter—but this time his horoscope from that day's newspaper was taped to the bottom:

> *TAURUS (April 20–May 20). Conditions are changing regarding your material interests, but you must work for what you receive. It's important that you don't waste time today on unproductive pursuits.*

Unfortunately, his letter was just that.

Then there was the guy who sent a form letter with a handwritten postscript on the bottom:

> *PS: 3/21/50, 3:33 AM, Youngstown, Ohio*

Others were not so brash:

> *Dear Shooting Star: I want you to know that I know little about astrology . . . but if you've got the skill I've the will—to teach and learn. I gather you are something between a fish and a ram . . . that is difficult for me to comprehend.*

and still other responses had that certain flair:

> *I'm a taurus in need of a compatible partner . . . not sure if rams and bulls make it but willing to investigate.*

and while some were humorous and warm:

How's a taurus? I'm not really all that bullish, but just enough. I've always had a certain feeling for rams.

I simply had to answer! A smile came to my face and my eyes lit up . . . for you see I am a generous affectionate Leo with Cancer rising. I like to think that the sensitive Cancer in me tempers many Leo traits which could otherwise get out of hand . . . therefore, I'm not a typical Leo but one with the best traits of both (but I suppose that kind of thinking is typically Leo, isn't it?). . . . I am interested in meeting a compatible Aries lady.

Others were a little *too* serious:

I am a Pisces born 32 years ago on Feb. 29 at 11:48 in the evening . . . in some ways I fit the typical Pisces mold yet in many ways depart sharply . . . would like to hear how you fit in depart as fate decree that our separate paths should cross for a possible common destination.

I think we have some things in common since I am also a Pisces born on the 23rd and express many Piscean traits in life and personality such as love of other people, great compassion for the needs of others, and have interest in certain fields of endeavor such as drama, teaching, which many Pisceans enter. Perhaps most of all, I am very intuitive and farsighted and can often visualize people and events that I have not yet met or experienced. Like most Pisceans, I am ultrasensitive and need a particular type of woman to interact with and who understands my sometimes differing preoccupied moods and need for affection. Per-

haps most of all I need a woman who will respect me and not see my "gift" of intuition as a "spooky" thing.

Oh my!
and some got carried away:

Greetings. I have a deep seeded [sic] interest in astrological matters and the way of foretelling the future. I'm an aquarian . . . and in regard to compatibility, I understand that Aries people and Aquarians are quite compatible. I consulted the I Ching in regard to same, the Khwei Hexagram states that 'notwithstanding the condition of things which it denotes, in small matters, there will be good fortune.' I perceive this to be a good sign and I await plotting future courses together.

OBJECT MATRIMONY

FEMALE (30), SEEKS SUPERIOR, professional, intelligent, strong-willed, obviously conceited and obnoxious, marriage-minded male with a sense of humor, wit, and originality that surpasses the average bore for usual courtship—object matrimony.

That describes my Mr. Right to a T; I've always liked men who like themselves. This ad brought out the best in people:

Dear modest and congenial! Your offer sounded so appealing, we both should take a better look. Attorney, never married, largely matching your checklist, wants to take a chance.

Hi, I'm a female who thought your ad was terrific. You and I have a lot of the same ideas about men.

If you should come across something only very decent and worthwhile and for some reason you can't accommodate, please pass along. Commissions, of course.

Hi, I'm George, very athletic, sensitive, caring, down-to-earth, witty, sexy, charming, intelligent, pro-athlete, secure emotionally and financially, dominant, yet gentle, 29 years young, single, no dependents, marriage-minded, creative, definitely superior, very good-looking, honest, conceited, and vain.

By this time you've received many letters from many guys, but like they say, leave the best for last . . . you say you're looking for a strong-willed, intelligent person who has a sense of humor and wits. Well, look no more, you lucky thing. You must be living right or went to church over the weekend because I really don't have to write to ads like this. Take a chance, Columbus did and look what he found.

Your interest in meeting someone conceited and obnoxious intrigues me. Most people find these traits to be less than charming; only a few of us appreciate their value. You must be a very perceptive and discriminating person. How long have you been undergoing treatment for this personality defect?

and the worst:

Dear 30-year-old female, your only description: If you are also very attractive—a professional yourself—secure in yourself, yet submissive and

*modest —can laugh at yourself and accept direc-
tion from a chauvinist, then call, my card's enclosed.*

Many of the respondents really got off on conceited, but
few admitted being obnoxious:

*I'm a 33-year-old male with many of the qualities
you seek. I'm extremely intelligent and knowledgeable, but I'm not overly obnoxious or conceited. Quiet confidence would be more like it.*

*I spotted your personal ad and I knew as a Leo I
had to respond. I'm all the things you asked except obnoxious. I have to be ungodly nice to
people all day, but after 5:00 I sometimes vent my
vileness. I am marriage-minded . . . ever since
my fiancée and I split over a year ago, I've been
pretty lost (she didn't appreciate my wit nor my
conceit). . . . Give me a call. As a strong-willed
person, I urge you to do so.*

*Dear Superior Seeker: O.K. as long as you're rea-
sonably attractive, you're on, but be warned. In
requesting superiority, intelligence, wit, originality, and humor. you may, this time, get exactly
what you've asked for. I don't merely surpass the
average bore for obviously if that were the case,
I'd be only an above average bore . . . I've never
been called obnoxious and have absolutely no as-
pirations along those lines.*

while others were obnoxious without even trying:

*Enclosed please find a picture. If this does not fill
the bill for conceit, I do not know what does. As
you can see, the conceit is well placed.*

I'm not quite certain I'm rotten enough to fill every one of your qualifications . . . I am not a bore, that much I know. I'm marriage-minded, but the chemistry must be there . . . I'm tired of feeding women's faces and getting the classic friendship speech, if you think you're special, I'll give you a chance.

Dear Searching for Superior Man: I fulfill your prerequisites with minor amendments: I'm honest and sincere, not conceited, and do not consider myself, nor am I considered, obnoxious. Furthermore, I'm good-looking . . . I strongly prefer a bright, personable, independent, pretty, slender, nonsmoking, professional woman who resides in an eastern suburb. Children, if any, should be at least of college age and emotionally independent of mother. I remain, Superior Man.

One guy signed this short note with a box number from his own ad:

I'm not sure about the obnoxious but I must be conceited because I'm quite certain I'm all the other things you're seeking. Box CM 8

and CM 8 read:

Screening test (female)—are you beautiful? intelligent? artistic? amorous? Athletic, 6' professional, wishes passing scores of 75% to send letter and phone.

Conclusion: For some reason, advertising for a conceited or obnoxious male gets you not only a high return but quality responses. I think it was the word "superior" that presented a challenge. Not responding to my ad would be like admitting one is not superior, thereby acknowledging a flaw in one's character.

Further conclusion: Egotists are screwed up but creative and intelligent.

EQUAL PERSUASION

INTELLIGENT, warm, nicely rounded woman (30), looking for playful, romantic, strong-willed, humorous Jewish male into daily gratification, laughter, and the good life. Innovative responses only.

What prompted me to place this ad was an impressive need to find solace with not just any man—but one my mother would approve of. I can now travel guiltless through life knowing I made the effort. I did my best and that is what counts. These were men not even a mother could love. They were

OVERCONFIDENT . . .

I perceive myself to be intelligent, warm, sensitive, and humanistic. Balancing my determination and resoluteness toward the more somber and sober concerns of life, I feel, is a sense of impulse and capriciousness toward life's lighter and more frivolous sides. My humor may not be too apparent in this letter, but being able to keep a whimsical touch on reality allows me to catapult myself across sometimes monotonous and mundane situations.

AND NOT SO . . .

. . . you are probably from Cleveburgh originally, so you probably know me, and if you so desire you have my explicit permission to crumple

this and try for basketball practice into the nearest receptacle.

INNOVATIVE . . .

Innovative—*obviously this word is derived from three roots:* **inn**—*a place for weary travelers to rest or dine;* **NOVA**—*a new occurrence, such as a dazzling star bursting forth into the firmament; and,* **votive**—*a gift, sometimes in the shape of a person. Internal literary evidence indicates that the above word calls for the following response: a meeting at a public place serving food with some-one new. Therefore, could we meet for a cup of coffee? I'll buy (that's the votive part).*

AND LACKING . . .

I was attracted to your ad in that it displayed both awareness and self-confidence. As for my traits that seem to match your needs, please call so that we may discuss same.

PRO-PRINCESS . . .

It is true what they say about Jewish men! And more . . . I'm a Jewish American prince with a hard to quit foot fetish willing to be a slave to your every gratification . . . providing you have golden arches and a well-turned ankle. . . . The Last of the Great Hebrew Lovers

AND ANTI . . .

I haven't met any Jewish women that attract me (yet), but I'm still looking. I don't smoke ciga-rettes, am not a heavy drinker but enjoy the com-pany of a sincere fun-loving female who is not into a house in the country, a Mercedes 450 SE coupe, and trying to continually outdo the Goldsteins. So if you think this guy is mensch enough for you, and you don't fly the flag of the rising sun, call me.

AS WELL AS INDIFFERENT . . .

I am not Jewish but I think I could be a good friend to you. I am on salary so I can get away for a couple of hours during the day.

HUMOROUS . . .

Friends regard me as handsome with an athletic build at 5'10" tall, 180 lbs., 34" waist, 10 fingers, and the same number of toes on each foot . . . a regular guy.

AND NON . . .

I am a Jew, slightly witty, but not a half-wit. . . . OK, enough humor . . .

MAN (31), single, Jewish, and verbose seeks female of same persuasion for sincere relationship

Cleveland being a small town persuasion-wise, almost everybody knows everyone else. But a few are new to the area, heavily sheltered or newly divorced, and they have not yet saturated the market.

I wrote this ad for my Jewish male friends and/or ex's. I hoped to bait those few new women and make them accessible.

I would like to meet you, if 1) you don't live at home; 2) you're not a member of JYSA; and 3) we've never met. Other than being Jewish, what would you like in a woman? I'm 1) in the business

world; 2) 5'5", slender; 3) Jewish and take judaism seriously; and 4) almost your age.

Your description seems extremely intriguing. Must be the word verbose, anyway, hi there, I'm of the same persuasion. I must tell you one thing: I abhor game playing. I consider myself an honest and sincere person and I'm tired of playing games. Life is too short and there are too many things to do.

If you are intelligent, refined, and good-looking (that also means overweight) then please call . . . I will listen to your verbosity.

. . . I am all the things you seek and much more. Positive attitude: 1) I voted for Nixon; 2) I'm willing to meet you; 3) I eat food with red dye #2. Integrity: 1) I never eat in a grocery store until after I've paid; 2) I work eight hours a day and don't punch a clock; 3) I'd rather lose than cheat. A warm heart: 1) I used to date a boy scout; 2) I have great aortic circulation; 3) I'm into public service work (note the halo). Intelligent: 1) properly educated; 2) smart enough to know to now end this letter. I like experimenting in the kitchen (that means changing light bulbs and rearranging the spice rack) and all aspects of living.

CATHOLIC FEMALE (early 20s) needs mature church-going guy for lasting, loving relationship. Must be into group functions, wafers, and early morning mass.

The most wholesome of my ads reaped the most wholesome of my responses. The friend for whom I placed this ad strongly recommends this mode of pursuit to those of the Catholic faith who are ISO (in search of).

From the delighted and those who could relate—

I was glad to see that there are still people who go to church and are interested in getting involved.

Dear Wonderful: So delighted to read your ad . . . I am a traditional Catholic who loves the mass and goes to early mass as it is such a joy . . . I love our holy Catholic Church so much! A woman who says as you do is such a joy, I hope I could meet you.

I too am a Catholic and am looking for someone of the same to enjoy a Christian way of life together . . . I do find enough time to worship the Lord at least twice a week and receive a great deal of satisfaction from his love within.

I thought to myself no one could appeal to me that would actually place an ad in a magazine. Then I turned to the back and came across yours. Your ad caught my eye because of the emphasis on religion. I'm not an evangelical or deeply pious man, but I do believe that God plays an important part in my life . . . I'm looking for someone with the same attitude. . . . I was born and raised near here and have nine brothers and sisters (I told you I was Catholic). I don't smoke or drink and wouldn't even consider using drugs. I have little patience with people who do.

to the skeptical (who wanted to relate but couldn't)—

*Saw your personal ad and it's refreshing to see an apparently moral person who isn't ashamed of the fact. . . . If you are **not** into dope, and don't smoke, perhaps we could get together and share some common praise of the Lord . . . altho I'm not ready for a serious personal commitment.*

*I worked my way through college stacking shelves . . . I belong to a parish where I'm a lay helper and take communion to the shut-ins in the neighborhood . . . if you like living, growing things, **are not a drug addict, or an alcoholic,** and are still interested, give me a call.*

to the serious—

I am looking for a beautiful shapely Christian woman who has never been married and has attributes like myself . . . I don't believe in divorce so I feel a dating relationship and engagement period of sufficient duration to really get to know one another, probably at least one full year, would be required. I'm emotionally starved and desirous for an intimate caring, sharing, steady relationship.

I don't know how early you like your mass, but I prefer the 11 AM mass. I don't go so much because of the time, but because for the community which is highly evident there. There's a lot of the spirit. To me, God has given me the gift, . . . it is through my work that I feel that I am a Christian doing what Christ wanted me to do. As a Catholic, I'm rather liberal. I don't automatically accept the church's rules and dogma. . . . As to group functions, I hope you mean church-related ones. I prefer a general mix of secular and spiritual . . . I love to view God's creation. Perhaps we can take in a mass together. May the Lord's peace go with you.

and to the perverted—

. . . I've been looking for a loving Catholic girl for some time . . . they have something special to give. I want you to know I'm thinking about what we can do this fall. You might find it strange that I would go to church regularly, and send you a letter like this—but I have met some horny, sexy girls during mass. I watch for one sitting alone and sit in the pew behind her and pretend she's doing the lewdest acts to me in her Sunday dress. Open up this spiritual card and you'll see how much I want you from the X-rated pictures enclosed. . . . PEACE BE WITH YOU.

ETHNIC ENTANGLEMENT

FEMALE (41), Italian, seeks male of same descent for traditional maid-oriented relationship. Do not answer unless you are a confirmed chauvinist, like to be waited on, and have never cleared the table.

Having dated an Italian man for several years, I've watched in disbelief while his mother and sister wait on him and his father hand and foot. After many discussions with women of Italian descent, it has become clear that this is the manner in which they were raised and they don't really mind being doormats. Therefore, when I was approached by a traditional Italian woman to write her an ad, I knew where to start. It worked:

I love to be waited on and have been called a chauvinist many times . . . if you are interested and we do hit it off, you can spoil me as much as you want.

Your ad is what I'm looking for in a woman. AMEN. I'm not Italian but like Italian women very much. I'm children, home, family and marriage minded to name a few.

I read your ad and would like you to meet my brother, John, for a blind date. He is also Italian. . . . John is college-educated, intelligent, kind, considerate, with good morals, and wants to get married. If you would like to meet him please phone me. Sincerely—Nancy.

*I am of Italian descent also and a little bit younger, tho I am seeking an older woman who can cater to **all** my needs. I believe that a woman, regardless of the age of her male counterpart, should satisfy her man in every way possible . . . emotionally I am very passionate and I like very passionate Italian women, especially if the woman will allow her man to lead as he should. I have nothing against a woman wanting to be equal, but in any male-female relationship, it should generally be the man who has more say in matters . . . since I've been well-acquainted with women much older, the oldest being 37, I can manage to make you feel **very** comfortable. I am also half-Greek in national origin—hope you don't mind.*

"CHAUVINIST OF THE YEAR"

I am Italian also and a physician. I would love to be waited on by you—Italian style—wearing a maid's outfit, black garters, black stockings, and heels. . . . At this time, the utmost of secrecy and discretion is needed for obvious reasons—if you need any of the apparel that I mentioned above, i.e., hose, garter belt—let me know.

MAY–DECEMBER–MAY

PROSPEROUS FEMALE (50ish), requires suitor (25–35), for adulation, adoration, admiration, and adulteration for December–May romance.

If you are or are planning to be a woman in your fifties, you'll be pleasantly surprised by this section. Literally thousands of men responded to the woman above for innumerable reasons—all wanting to act out their fantasies with this more than cooperative female.

I am sure I was not alone in my belief that older men were better off in the romance category than older women. I never realized that so many men would be anxious to pursue a relationship (full-time, part-time, and overtime) with an older woman. (That's an understatement—*they're on their knees!*) As a matter of fact, I think I'll be better off at fifty than I am at thirty.

The men who replied were from all walks of life . . .

Some were insulted by my age requirements—

I would like to know the difference between 39 years old and your preferred age of 25–35.

What can a 25–35-year-old man do that I can't? I am 55 and can bowl all day long.

and others paid no attention—

First let me tell you that I am 38. I know this is the top of your age range requirement scale but I can pass for several years younger.

Your ad calls for a suitor 25 and up but I'm only 22. I have gone out with girls two years older and younger than me.

I am 36 years old (one over the limit) and am a successful executive with LOTS of free time.

I wonder if his boss knows?
Some had their own requirements—

I would hope that you are a youthful, attractive, and vibrant woman.

I am very interested in meeting a lady who is fifty years YOUNG. . . . I know I can supply you with the better feelings we all enjoy and need as I am very willing to please you.

and only one admitted to questionable performance—

I am 52 and am not sure I could act like a 30-year-old but if it makes a difference, I'm clean, healthy, and have had a vasectomy.

Many men didn't understand the term "December–May"—

I guess it's fate but I was born in May so I guess I am half your May–December relationship.

Am available December thru May.

I am very worldly and fairly prosperous myself . . . do we really have to wait until December?

Actually I was hoping for something a touch closer to Halloween.

I am young, tall, lean, and striking and can easily fulfill your 4 A's; call me anytime, why wait until December?

while many got off on it—

After ten years of marriage to a woman seven years younger than myself and two years of chasing women, I find that a mature woman is more to my liking.

They seem so mature . . . you are probably more mature and more of a woman . . . an older woman like yourself could show me how a lady likes to be loved.

Your age is your attraction. I would like to share my successes and failures with a woman older than I.

and a few could hardly conceal their excitement—

I was very turned on by your ad. . . . I don't smoke or take drugs . . . female companionship is MY drug. . . . I'm a one-woman man and I'm in shape.

I love to hang out at the beach in my bikini and check out the scene . . . I'm into nude sunbathing on a private beach or on my own boat . . . I enjoy posing and giving sensual massage . . . I have brown hair (including chest hairs) . . . I'm having a marvelous time writing to you and I wish you could see me now.

Having read your ad nearly an hour ago, I must confess that even yet I am fully aroused.

I desire to engage in sensually provocative correspondence, to share in your desire and to share mine . . . hope that you enjoy full arousal like I am right now.

the fantasy aspect was too much to bear—

I like your fantasy as I have personally experienced a similar one 10 years ago in Southern France . . . adulteration is nice.

Your ad stimulated a fantasy of mine that I would like to become reality.

Dear Master: I am looking for a female master—one for which I can do openly all the things you ask. I have often fantasized being able to give myself in adoration to an older woman but have never had the nerve to let it be known. . . . I am a good-looking professional and would welcome becoming your personal servant and maid . . . to perform any bidding or command which you might desire for however long you wish to retain me.

Some were in praise of older women—

Mature single women have a rough time today . . . everybody is out to rip them off, swinger clubs, mail-order companies, porn peddlers, models, everybody. . . . I sincerely feel they deserve more sex and happiness than the average young woman because they've paid their dues.

You sound like a woman who knows what she wants out of life. I like being with an older woman mainly because a woman older is better in many ways; smarter about life and takes better care of herself. . . sexually mature . . . knowing how to treat a man.

others wanted to show it—

Adulteration, we should work at together . . . I'll supply the 'adulation, adoration, and admiration' . . . sexually I'm strong but gentle . . . I make sure my partner is always satisfied.

I've always dreamt about an older woman to 'adore, admire, and adulterize' . . . I am in my early 20s tho varying circumstances have matured me beyond my 21 years while still leaving me with a yet-to-be released youthful virility . . . you'll find me a wonderful LOVING sort.

Not pretending to be macho but I never find it difficult to attract females as you can see from my nude photo . . . if nothing evolves from this letter I'll still consider it a thrill . . . you must be one hell of a woman.

and there were two with a "different" quality—

I hope you're not married; if you are, throw this number away because I don't want any trouble with any jealous husband.

Oh, I want to meet you. I loved your ad. Please call me OR MY ROOMMATE LOVER at home or at work.

OLDER MEN are worldly, distinguished, self-assured, discerning, and dignified. Won't you humor a young woman (mid-20s) with a gallant attempt at romance?

Webster's Dictionary defines gallant as nobly chivalrous and often self-sacrificing, courteously and elaborately attentive especially to ladies, given to amorous intrigue. Who wouldn't want a man of this description? Add some years of experience and savoir faire, a touch of sophistication and some self-assurance, and you can't go wrong.
The men agree—

> *Your knowledgeable ad prompted me to respond. . . . I am a very young 50 and have had a distinguished career . . . I am an incurable romantic and am looking for that sensitive, lovely, intelligent woman that your ad indicates you are. . . . I love good food, wine, and clothes and also love horseracing—I have sometimes suggested to my friends that great racehorses and some women have something in common—it's called CLASS. . . . I would be privileged to meet you and earn the right to project my 'gallant attempt at romance' (what beautiful phrasing).*

> *I agree totally with your ad in the magazine received today. . . . I am very selective as females go, but easy to get along with . . . striking and distinguished.*

Some tried to convince me they were older—

> *Merely the act of responding to your ad makes me feel older. In fact, I can feel my arteries harden.*

*Fred Astaire married the woman of his dreams
and I do hope I am as lucky as he.*

while others weren't sure—

*I don't know what you mean by 'older men' —
older than mid-20s? I would love to humor you
with a gallant attempt (altho I don't make attempts) at romance.*

*I am a single male, 40 years of age. In your opin-
ion is that too young to be worldly, distinguished,
self-assured, discerning, and dignified?*

*I am not sure how old you're looking for —most of
my hair is still blond (what's left of it) and I am
definitely older than you.*

To some, age wasn't a factor—

*I'm 42 and can disco all night . . . I have been
known to cry at weddings, brake for animals, and
always stay at home on Halloween for trick-or-
treat. . . . I believe foreplay is more important
than the energy crisis and I caress not molest.*

*Loved your ad, but the real test of a 50-year-old
man is if he can still run out three-base hits and
not need oxygen.*

but some were old before their time—

*I'm a Sagittarius, a 1976 college graduate,
Catholic (you'll get over it), and the fourth of
eight children. All the rest were normal.*

*Ah, yes. To be mature and worldly is an awesome
burden to carry on one's shoulders . . . well,*

since you have asked, I accept your invitation to learn about these concepts—I'm 29 and oh so gallant.

while some scoffed at the word "attempt"—

Gallant attempt?? Don't you know when us men become older we become better in many ways? We know how to be sensitive, loving, and sensuous.

I would not have to humor you, because I would not have to attempt romance. I am romantic by nature.

others needed a fail-safe technique—

*I am 50, in good health; financially okay and willing to **compensate** for a really good time with a discreet **knowledgeable** gal.*

and others relied on their sense of humor to get by—

I'm 37, that makes me older—the capital of Tibet is Lhasa and that makes me worldly—young ladies are more fun and adventuresome and that makes me discerning—I like Halston cologne— does that make me dignified or distinguished?

I'M AN EX- (DEPENDENTS WELCOME?)

DIVORCED male would like to meet female of same status for "war story" exchange and soothing battle scars.

Is it one out of three or two out of three marriages that end in divorce today? Many times I feel like an outsider at parties, beaches, and supermarkets. Let's not kid ourselves, divorce is a major topic of discussion—each person thinking his or her story is worse than the next.

> *War hero: I've also been thru a battle. If the battle wasn't too gory, I'm willing to listen. I too have battle scars—maybe ours match?*

> *I'd be glad to hear your war stories and soothe your battle scars but mine are pretty well-healed . . . are you Caucasian or Christian?*

> *If you're feeling down about your divorce, I can have you up and laughing in no time. I'm a recent divorcée and have almost totally recovered and hidden my battle scars, not an easy task . . . daytime soap operas are battling to use my war stories for their story lines . . . they're that bizarre.*

There were a few Nurse Nightingales who wanted to minister to my friend's needs for the possibility of a future healthy existence—

> *I'm neither married nor divorced but a very good listener with a first-aid kit. If you're still looking for a good shoulder and TLC, happy to help out . . . Lisa's Crises Control Center*

> *Dear Divorced Male with Bleeding Wounds in Need of Soothing: if you're interested in charm, wit, and all the rest of the flowers of womanhood, let me know . . . however, if we meet, let's not swap each other's war stories—let's begin a whole new war story which won't have any battle*

scars . . . a chance to begin a new story based on trust, caring, sharing, and all other things that were perhaps missing before.

Dear Veteran: From the sound of your ad you appear to have been recently wounded. Possibly still suffering from shell shock? I find the ad void of anger which is a good sign. I trust that you are not bitter about this previous battle. Enough said. I'm not into premasticated answers that fit into the back pockets of the bar scene players' designer jeans. Then again, I'm not into pseudointellectual conversations that lead nowhere except to boredom and little to be remembered the next morning when brushing my teeth . . . or the transparent relationships that rarely last past the bad breath the next morning brings. If you're looking for more than a convenient waterbed to fall into on an irregular basis, then consider a late phone call and see where it takes you.

I'M DIVORCED (who isn't?), late 30s with kids, a German shepherd, and a big house. Need male companionship—the dog just isn't enough.

When I was approached by a thrice-divorced friend of mine to help her in her quest for the fourth and final, I had a little trouble going about it in a serious fashion (and believe me, she was *serious*). Although she felt the levity of the last phrase was a bit *too*, it resulted in a healthy and original group of responses:

If you're still looking for male companionship, please call—I know I can do better than the dog.

I'm applying for the position as replacement for your German shepherd on a part-time basis. I appreciate a woman who is mature and knows the facts of life.

Your ad didn't say what you and the shepherd are doing. A shepherd could be a tough act to follow.

I love kids and German shepherds but I love their mistress and mother even more!

I've never applied to take the place of a dog before, but it sounds like fun.

You're right—somehow even Rin Tin Tin couldn't do it all, but maybe I can . . . I admit I've never been married and I don't chase bones but for you I could be witty and warm, hoping to take over where Rin Tin Tin left off.

Am divorced too, no dog, need female compansionship—the dogs I meet just aren't enough.

Some of our male counterparts are still hung up on that ancient stereotype of a divorced woman—a "pushover."

I'm also late 30s, no kids, no dog, just a stable good-looking businessman with ALL the optional equipment necessary.

White male, 32, warm, affectionate, and super in bed, happily married but looking for some extra play . . . I have flexible hours, am quiet and soft-spoken but am strictly good time . . . give it a shot.

If you're adventuresome and think you can handle a 'younger one,' give me a call . . . bet you can't.

I'm single, unattached, a physician and dare say rather good-looking . . . I must confess that neither the dog or house interest me but I would indeed be interested in a relationship based on physical satisfaction.

And then some were just, well, you know:

You are right, a dog isn't enough. I have two cats, Samatha and Taboo, and as much as I love them, I need a non-furry, non-four-footed tailless creature to talk to . . . I was just telling that to Taboo this evening as we sat watching the sun go down.

I'm not divorced since I've never been married. I'm not fond of kids though I love animals. I dislike German shepherds and tend to believe people who own them are paranoid. At this point, you are probably asking why this guy even bothered to write? Sometimes you have to play a hunch even if the facts don't add up. Maybe it was the big house part or the comfortable unabashed humor. Anyhow, give me a call and let's see what wins out—logic or intuition!

I'm uninhibited, yet discreet (on Tuesdays and Thursdays); I'm Caucasian with blond hair that I wear Kojak style; I enjoy music of all kinds, dancing, cooking, stimulating conversation, and dirty

*movies; but most of all, I enjoy spending time with
an intelligent companion who has an excellent, if
somewhat bizarre, sense of humor.*

SUGAR DADDY REQUESTED

VERY ATTRACTIVE single female (24), seeks
SUGAR DADDY. Guaranteed full commitment and
confidentiality and more, no matter what your obli-
gations; that's compensation for setting me up in the
style I'm accustomed to. QUALIFICATIONS EX-
CHANGED.

After hearing of my personal ad-writing abilities, a
friend of mine requested that I assist a friend of hers in
finding a sugar daddy. She had not been able to afford
to finish college and was now having a hard time pay-
ing her bills. She was desperate. I tried long and hard to
talk her out of this crazy idea. I warned her that her $50
investment would be wasted, that no man would dare
respond to such an outlandish request.

She is now attending college while living a life of
leisure, and I'm still living in "plasticized" debt.
From wealthy and healthy:

*I'm a doctor looking for an extramarital relation-
ship. I would like at my expense to meet with you.
To show my honesty, please allow me to purchase
some new clothes for you at our first meeting.
Even if we cannot work things out—so to
speak—at least you will know I am not cheap and
have good intentions. Interested?*

*What are your qualifications? I'm 5'9", 37, with
curly hair and beard, professional and slim, but
with other LARGE attributes.*

I'm responding to your ad. I have a 30' sailboat, and own a race car and just leased a new Buick. Already this year I have been to Florida and California . . . I also know where you're coming from.

to worldly and wise:

The situation you are looking for is one that I have been involved with before. However, at the present time, I have no real commitment . . . I am willing to provide security . . . write and send photo.

Depending on what your exact demands and specifications are, I could have just what you are looking for. If you want to have fun and make tax-free money, WRITE.

to healthy, wealthy, worldly, and wise:

I am a professional man in the medical field who is very good-looking . . . up-front and honest, devoting myself to mine and others' fantasies and sexual fulfillment . . . my main concern and what pleases me most is the pleasure received by the woman. Your wish is my every command and desire. I am very versatile and uninhibited and in exchange for a large apartment, money, and food, you could make me very, very happy . . . follow through—I'm for real!

the offers kept right on coming:

I am in no position to "set you up" and know that your SUGAR DADDY will get sour after a while . . . after you're set, I'd like to keep your life and mind sweet when you're bored and need to be refreshed.

I responded over a month ago and never received a response . . . if you have found a SUGAR DADDY at least let me know . . . perhaps you have a friend who's interested in the same arrangement?

I hope you are not using that word VERY ATTRACTIVE loosely . . . I own my own business and live in a house NOT AN APARTMENT.

DISCRETION ADVISED

Married woman (early 30s) looking for discreet playmate (attached or un-) for adventurous romping and total fulfillment. NO STRINGS.

In less than two weeks more than 2,000 men responded to this ad. Never did I imagine the effect this ad would have on the magazine I placed it in, nor did the married woman who participated. Within a month ads popped up plagiarizing my ad to advertise for a mistress—

Married professional man (early 40s) attractive and kind is looking for an attractive playmate for most nights, for intimate and totally fulfilling relationship with no involvement.

More incredible than the number of responses were the responses themselves. Doctors wrote on their prescription pads, lawyers sent fake subpoenas, and with absolutely no discretion. I received theater tickets, dinner coupons, dinner invitations, dimes pasted to letters to pay for phone calls, stamps for return letters, photos, business cards, post cards, and promises of boat trips, airplane trips, and other kinds of trips I won't discuss here. There wasn't one man (and the responses now number over 10,000) who didn't describe his physical attributes and his competence as a lover.

From horny

> *I read your ad seeking an explicit "afternoon relationship." This strikes a cordant note in my "horny heart" . . . no inhibitions . . .*

> *. . . I am unattached, have plenty of free time, a place to romp and am always horny . . . the girls say I'm pretty good looking, 180 pounds, not fat just stocky.*

and well-hung

> *. . . while I have a large ego I feel odd giving a verbal description . . . I am an attorney and sexually active, well-hung with great stamina.*

> *. . . if an attractive, generously endowed, middle-aged Jewish gentleman for your discreet playmate sounds interesting, this one would enjoy hearing from you.*

> *I am a 32 year old caucasian male who is well-endowed (I'm told). I enjoy the challenge of "romping" with married women.*

to I don't know what

> *Oh, I'm your man . . . I'm willing to play any game you can name or invent . . . I am into French and Greek! I love to love and be loved. I dig sexy women and love to photograph them nude or in sexy panty, bra and high hills [sic], garter belts and black stockings. I believe strongly in being discreet.*

letters came from those experienced

> *I was destined for unusual romance. I don't consider myself to be any kind of gigolo but for some damn reason some of my best relationships have been with women who also happen to be someone else's ladies . . . and I still live to write to you now.*

> *I'm your man! I've probably forgot more about romping and total fulfillment than a lot of men will ever know. Not bragging, just facts, Mam! Been married three times and now on fourth and about to shed her! I've had enough mistresses that I can't even remember all their names and the one nighters I can't even count! Not bragging, just facts, Mam!*

> *I like adventurous romping and could relate some stories to you about being on beaches, highschool bleachers, park paths, night swimming, etc., however, you may be more interested in you and I . . . I'm into massage and jog nude three times a week 12 –16 miles*

> *If you want a few references as to whether I can satisfy, I can give you a few phone numbers to call and these ladies will verify all I have said. I am into oral sex also if you dig it. I'm not into S&M and don't think I can handle it . . . I never get enough sex.*

and those not

> *I would be very good at being your playmate because I don't smoke or take drugs. As a result,*

I'm highly sexed . . . I'm honest and I'll show you now. I have the knowledge and the tools, however, I lack experience. This is to your advantage, tho, because you could train me to your own taste, delights and pleasures.

If you're talking of having some fun with no commitments, I'm interested. What would be more adventurous and interesting than having a 19 year old virgin as your playmate? I have some young new ideas and would be willing to try.

some were surprised

Frankly, I was surprised that any woman would want such an arrangement but anything is possible. . . . I've often thought it is a shame that our society limits us to one intimacy per lifetime.

and some were confused

Your biggest decision will be which one and how many . . . also where? The how should take care of itself! How do I get high priority? How will you choose? If it makes a difference . . . I'm a white collar worker and able to pay most of my bills most of the time (and I've had a vasectomy!).

I'm curious to know what prompted you to place the ad?? Are you ugly? Why did you ad 'total fulfillment'? Are you horny? Does your husband know about this? Where will you keep the mail? What if your husband replies? Don't you wish you asked for $1 each? Will you call, will you write? Do you have any idea of the thoughts running thru my head?

but most were excited

> *This will be a first in ten years of marriage. . . .
> I'm excited to say the least; I'll probably do my
> best work of the year today just thinking about
> you.*

> *Having read your ad nearly two hours ago, I must
> mention I am fully aroused . . . my mind envi-
> sions you to be full of flame, kindled with passion
> overflowing, eager, seductive and responsive.*

> *I have endurance. I just need someone who knows
> how to keep a guy going. I could go on and on but
> I would get too excited. And that's not as good as
> flesh, touching and kissing, whispering and talk-
> ing, laughing and stroking can be.*

Although claims of discretion did occur

> *I am unattached and my friends think overly dis-
> creet.*

> *I can be as discreet as you want to be. This is why
> the phone number I leave for you to call is from a
> pay phonebooth . . . and that is why I should be
> your playmate.*

> *I can be discreet too. For instance, when we go
> out to dinner, I'll wear a black overcoat, upturned
> collar, dark glasses and a wide brim hat. . . . I
> think we'll have a great time dodging here and
> there and I'm willing to go along with the deal,
> believe me!*

> *If it's a discreet playmate you're looking for, then
> you'll appreciate the brown envelope!*

Discreet?? Figure out who you're going to be and give me some number, any number to call . . . I know . . . you be Lois Lane and I'll be Clark Kent.

and some carried it to an extreme (at a high cost to me)

Run an ad in the magazine saying "Hey, play-mate, call me" and give me information on how to contact you.

Before commencing, I think a phone conversation would be best to acquaint ourselves. If you would please place an ad in the paper as follows: "ST—please call" with phone number and time and sign your box number, we can take it from there. Discreet enough?

others weren't sure how to go about it

I live in a small town less than an hour from you and it is difficult to discreetly romp locally.

but gave it the proverbial college try

I was voted most likely to have a discreet relation-ship with a married woman in her early 30s by the senior class seven years ago.

Many men blamed a bad marriage

I've wanted to do exactly what you've done, put an ad in and look for someone to bring some love and laughter back in my life . . . things between my wife and I have changed . . . having fun is forced and arguments are frequent. I want happi-ness and sincerity before it's too late.

I'm ready for you . . . I'm married and bored to death . . . Call. If my wife answers, hang up!

others didn't bother

> *I'm 36, married and want to stay that way.*

but all agreed they wanted to get the most out of life

> *I'm self employed and own a bake shop. You're saying "Oh No!," a fat old baker . . . not true. . . . Your ad reminds me of myself. I also enjoy the adventure of life.*

> *I'm not married. I'm living with the woman who I've lived with for years. We met because I was adventurous, she was married at the time. I just want to add here I didn't want to break up their marriage . . . just in case it worries you.*

and were glad I did too

> *I do not normally respond to these requests; however, your outlook on life caught my eye.*

> *It is rare to find a person who wants the most out of life. I would like to be your PERMANENT discreet playmate.*

Others had their own reasons

> *I too am looking for this type of relationship. . . . I'm a lawyer, living alone in the Heights. My wife lives in Rochester (where I occasionally commute) each pursuing separate professional careers . . . this would be a first. No bullshit!*

> *My professional dealing with ladies is making them beautiful . . . in other words, I am a hairstylist. I enjoy beautiful lady's presents [sic].*

I also am married and looking for the same fun and fulfillment. If you're not interested, too bad for both of us, burn photo and have fun.

I look forward to being playmates . . . I always wanted a playmate . . . we can play house where you would be the woman, of course, and I the man. We could take a bath and go beddy-bye.

I'm 31, single and have a nicely decorated apartment.

To be honest with you, I'm not getting enough.

Yes, I'm married too. My wife has a career of her own—an all consuming passion. Need I say more?

and made their own demands

*I am a very physical person and enjoy a woman who likes to be loved **well** for I am a skillful and passionate love maker . . . otherwise don't call.*

If I'm good enough to please you then you would have to keep the relationship between you and I to keep the chances of getting VD next to impossible. My girl wouldn't like it nor would your husband.

MISTRESS (ONCE REMOVED)

HOT POTATO, recently dropped (vocation—mistress), needs to be rescued by attached male who needs permanent outside diversion. No monetary obligation.

What an arrangement for both parties. There are plenty of women who are more than happy with a once or twice a week rendezvous—hold the laundry. And when it comes to free sex, well, let some of the two thousand-plus men who responded to my friend speak for themselves—

> *You should be hearing the thunder of the approaching cavalry coming to your rescue! Or you might be hearing the clashing of armor as I approach on my gallant steed. And if you listen carefully, the sound of my sword unsheathing as I prepare to battle dragons. . . . I'm "attached" (euphemism for married) at present.*

> *I swear with an ad like that you'll no doubt get three quarters of Ohio on your doorstep all ready to rescue you and, oh, daughter, I wish you well . . . I suspect you would be a plus to anyone's life . . . I would be happy to rescue you. I feel that is what I'm here for. I'm not the best-looking fellow, but I am clean.*

Responses came in from potato connoisseurs who ran hot—

> *Call for some deep fried fun.*

cold—

> *Your recent ad caught my eye and was too good to pass up. I'm looking for a playmate and would like to know more. Please respond soon there is nothing worse than a cold potato.*

and luke—

Let's get mashed together.

All of whom were interested in this rescue effort—

This is a first but my earlier childhood has me conditioned to rescue the young ladies.

Couldn't help feeling for someone who needs rescuing. It took courage to write what you did and you just might be one heck of a woman . . . I am a businessman 6'3" tall with 225 pounds (all man) evenly molded over a strong athletic frame. A former athlete, am extremely healthy, virile, and well built in every way.

I hope you can read my writing as I'm on a plane to Chicago and the seats don't afford much room. Your ad caught my eye and by now you must have received a thousand letters. . . . I really need some type of outside diversion and would gladly come to your rescue.

I am a 33-year-old knight to rescue you and allow you to fill your vocation. . . . Believe it or not, I'm married 18 years and enjoy outside diversion. . . . I'm not against the touch of the grape, a puff of the weed, or in general a good mellow time. I jog 30 miles a week. P.S. I believe all age groups have something to offer.

whether they were attached—

In answer to your ad I hope you're what I'm looking for. I had an ex-friend lover for seven years.

*This ended a year ago. Since then, I've been with other women and feel I'm ready to seek a lasting relationship with someone who will enjoy an honest sincere and comforting period of time together with me. I enjoy sex, love to teach and be taught new ways of enjoyment, but I **do not** and **will not** be in competition for you. If it's right, it's right, if it's not, no loss. By the way, I'm happily married with three children.*

I've been married since May of 1978 and have been close to a couple of affairs already but to go about one like this really adds to the excitement. . . . We've been lucky, no kids, but with our sex life that is no surprise.

My case is probably different from most letters you've received. I'm not married but I am attached—to my job. I'm self-employed and have been so busy that my social life has gone right down the tubes.

or un—

Unfortunately, I am an unattached male in his 40s but your ad intrigued me so much I had to write. Unattached males need outside diversion too and in fact there are probably advantages to the unattached variety. . . . Not only that but your vocation as mistress sounds most romantic . . . could you make just this one exception and call me.

Am terribly curious why only attached? Unattached men love and need same things. If you're attractive or reasonably so . . . call and let's discuss the matter. Am together with all the normal equipment. Situation can be as permanent as you like . . . if I like.

Although some needed convincing as to authenticity—

Professional man with college degree. Good income, well settled. Will travel 50-mile radius. No cheapskate but was interested in your description of no monetary obligation because it took you out of the commercial category. Incidentally, I'm not a baldy. I've juggled a few hot potatoes in my career but I never have dropped one. Excuse self-typing as secretary mustn't know. Understand?

and some were curious—

After you've tried all your other responses write me, but not before. I'm not in the market for a mistress. Have several friends now who take care of my needs, but I must admit I'm curious. I always thought I experienced everything. Evidently not.

Your ad is hard to believe, but I am curious —not yellow.

others were into "outside diversion"—

Boy do I need outside diversions. I'm good-looking, stable, and have all the optional equipment necessary to engage in a hot romance with all the frills.

Just got back from Morocco trying to lead a romantic life on camel back—but you seem like the perfect diversion instead.

I am desperate for an exciting diversion to take me away from all of this ho-hum. If you are searching for just another guy, throw this letter away. If you feel chained to a tree with dragons on all quarters, drop a reply in the mail 25 words or less about you, your life, your hopes and desires. You may not get a Pulitzer, but you'll get my return call.

Some really got into this mistress thing—

I am a Gemini (Geminis make the best lovers) and between mistresses (my latest moved to Arizona when her husband was transferred). I am clean, discreet, housebroken, educated, and a self-employed person who can meet days, evenings, weekends and can travel with you to many places. Do you wish to be taken out to lunch and/or dinner weekly, biweekly, every other day, every day??

I have much time to enjoy. But married and tied tight because of business and property.

You said your vocation was mistress. That sounds exciting to me. I need your expertise. Most mistresses are expert lovers, are you? I know I am.

I would like to meet you very much. Yes I need extra outside diversion but you can be assured that I would be your closest and dearest friend. You would know all my intimate secrets and I am sure you would let me cry on your shoulder. P.S. I'm married.

You should change your vocation, probably to advertising. Your ad is a masterpiece for creating interest and intrigue for what it says and what it

*doesn't say. My compliments. I'll try to respond
in kind preserving some semblance of anonymity:
Vichysoisse, recently chilled, vocation miscreant,
needs to be warmed by detached female who
needs prominent inside perversion. (Sorry, I tried
to avoid such obvious sexual reference but all the
good variations on your ad reach the same results.)*

including a few carrot danglers—

*I am a financial and tax specialist. I am a multi-
interested person and have been known to take my
lady friends to Vegas for long weekends if they can
get away.*

*I have dated other females through ads in other
publications. Each time they were based upon a
financial arrangement and lasted for a fair
amount of time. I usually spend between $300 and
$500 a month on my outside activities, but that's
all I can comfortably afford and support. I only
outline this to give you an idea of my status.*

but some were interested only in sex—

*I would treat you like a queen. I would be a good
lover. I am clean, safe, well-endowed, and
lasting.*

*Having been a boy scout some years ago, I
earned merit badges in lifesaving and first aid and
would like to attempt rescue. . . . I am currently
residing with the female companion I've had for
several years and her cat. Despite the possible
similar references, both soft, and cudly, the sharing of such attributes is waning as is conversation*

and other oral endeavors . . . consequently, I should like to offer myself as a buoy in the steamy frustrated dampness of your dilemma and hopefully bring you to higher climatic shores. Perhaps you can also bring to me a newfound buoyancy, purpose, and sense of direction. Talents I have acquired include auto repair and I feel confident in conversation on this and other subjects. So if you should feel stimulated to respond and have a need or desire for a gentle carburetor adjustment or if your choke is somewhat sticky and you'd like it thoroughly cleaned; and/or fluids checked, please call some evening to make further arrangements.

Very interested in your proposal. One of us is 36, 6' tall, 189 pounds, the other is 33, 6'2", 183 pounds. Both of us are business executives.

How about giving me a try. I'm sure I have the right kind of cream for your hot potato, believe me, it's anything but sour . . . several years ago I got into body building. Ever since then I've never been so sexually excited . . . the more I exercise, the hornier I get.

Hi. I have brown hair and eyes, a hairy body, and am well-hung (9" × 6" round) . . . I enjoy straight and French and honestly enjoy pleasing a female to the utmost degree. Satisfaction guaranteed.

Where have you been for 32 years. I started late in life, age 9. You are just what I need. Please call before I go blind.

ROOMMATE WANTED

WOMAN (27) seeks roommate to share bed and board. One bed, one bored.

I placed this ad for myself. It generated a surprisingly small number of responses, but they weren't boring.

ROOMMATE—

My name is Carl and I want to move out cause I'm bored as hell . . . I'm friendly, charming and I don't snore.

I'm 35, self-employed, I would make a good roommate as I'm very neat. I always put the cap back on the toothpaste.

I'm not a gay person nor am I a woman beater.

I will share your bed and pay all the board. Your worries are over.

How many girls these days want an up front relationship and are willing to say so? I've been looking for a female roommate —let's face it, it's sure better than another guy. I don't want to be crass, but I'll state I'm considerate and good. You'd be satisfied with me and also warm on those cold winter nights. Plans look good for my future so you wouldn't have to worry about my half of the rent.

PLAYMATE—

If we shared a bed, you'd never be bored.

You're right, one bed and one bored can get boring, but it could be worse—two beds and two bored. I will say that many find me romantic and funny . . . in bed I get pleasure from giving pleasure . . . I have experience where it counts and very few hang-ups. You can share my king coil, and I'll share your beautyrest.

Your ad is cute but rather evasive. I'm somewhat intrigued. Are you seeking a male, female, or doesn't it make any difference? If you're impartial as far as sex standards are concerned, then I can only assume that you may be bisexual. If by some chance you're into swinging, my lady friend would like to get together with you. I don't know if you've ever been in a threesome, but I can assure you it's a lot of fun. I've always fantasized seeing two women together and when I finally did see it WELL! We're both attractive, clean, and discreet. Think about it and give me a call if you're game.

CHECKMATE—

I would like to discuss sharing your board with you even though I will not be able to live with you . . . in return, I would like to see you one or two afternoons during the week.

You state that you are seeking someone to share a bed and board . . . the board I could share totally, the bed I could share occasionally . . . if we were compatible, you would find I could give much more than I would ask in return.

EXECUTIVE SUITE

FEMALE EXECUTIVE (30), needs male companionship for moviegoing, antiquing, warm friendship, and finishing my leftovers.

The term "executive" has a strange effect on people when used in relation to the opposite sex (either one). There is an aura surrounding "executives"—they are automatically thought to be aggressive, authoritative, and successful.

Many of my responses were from executive men who sought an executive woman because of their own professional status, while other writers were threatened and intimidated by a female of this stature. Then there were the few who *savored* being walked on (especially by an executive) . . .

From submissive—

> *I need a relationship with a sensual aggressive woman.*

> *I am well-educaded [sic] and considered very good-looking . . . I have a strong need for female companionship . . . I can appricate [sic] and believe in female rights and have always been submissive in nature to an aggressive female . . . if upon meeting we find that we are compadible [sic], I would be more than happy to eat your leftovers or anything els [sic] that you might desire me to eat.*

to hostile—

> *I sincerely hope that you are not seeking someone to beg you for a relationship.*

You challenge me to convince you that I'm the man you're looking for . . . I'm not even going to try. If there's any convincing to be done, it'll be done by you . . . I have enough confidence in myself to say "accept me as I am."

From true executives—

We may independently meet at a preselected place for coffee, conversation, and the opportunity to become acquainted . . . anything additional will be on mutual agreement at heretofore stated meeting . . . after all we executives must work in unison . . . SRE: Mo.

to executive material—

I'm thinking of enrolling in a school for interior designing, but I'm uncertain whether it will clash with my other life as a professional entertainer.

some were impressed with me—

The reason your ad caught my eyes is because of your title. I have managed to save a nice piece of money to open a business . . . I would like to keep in touch with someone who is willing to take a little time out to share a few ideas with me that will help me invest my money in the right business that will pay off in the long run . . . I am sure you have knowledge in that department.

some were impressed with themselves—

Last week I 'bought' a seat at the Repertory Cinema, which means they will stick a brass plaque with my name on it on a seat of my choice. This appealed to my vanity.

some were not impressed at all—

My big dislikes are phony, showy people, wearing suits and ties.

and some couldn't care less—

I am moviegoing and I am an antique . . . I adore leftovers and some of them are my best friends.

Because of my success with the executive ad, I placed a similar one for a friend of mine who's a lawyer.

GOOD HUMOR MAN (35), attorney, seeks classy, nice-looking woman for indoor and outdoor fun.

A high number of quality responses indicated that many women aren't opposed to spending more time with an executive of another kind—an attorney (moreover, one with a sense of humor and an appreciation of someone classy) . . .

I definitely qualify in the classy, good-looking category and require a man with the same specs . . . maybe a conversation will tell.

Definitely classy—know what I mean??? Own diamonds, gold, furs, and wardrobe to match . . . I'm more indoor than out depending on what the latter includes . . . my choice is the best without fail.

I'm pretty, sexy, depraved, and live alone. I'm feeling rather shy—what if we turn out to loathe one another? I'm 30 but frequently taken for 22 and have recently been told I am the most disconcerting and classy woman the speaker has ever known—also the most inteligent [sic] and the most fascinating. Who are you?

I'm age 33, with classic features, single, red hair, blue eyes, and not a terrific typist . . . men are very often unhappy because women tell them in letters they are better looking and turn out to be bowsers. SO, I won't promise gorgeous—only NOT BAD AT ALL.

ATHLETICALLY INCLINED?

INTERNATIONALLY KNOWN professional athlete (male 31) with business and social ties in [this area] seeks appropriate lady who can handle "life in the fast lane."

An "internationally known professional athlete"? Run for the perfumed stationery. Although credit for this ad must go to one of my friends, it was a great surprise to this athlete when he suddenly started receiving letters in the mail. The ad and its responses were a birthday present to him. Women of all sorts responded to the ad, most being into an incredible amount of sports, all being supergorgeous according to their own descriptions, adding up to the largest response I have ever seen to a male ad of this type . . .

From fast lanes—

I'm a fun-loving lady who has had experience with fast lanes; being 18 doesn't necessarily portray character or naiveté.

I must tell you that 'life in the fast lane' really aroused my interest due to the fact that I'm what most people refer to as a moving violation.

to slow lanes—

> *My life is definitely a slow lane ramble and the only internationally known people dear to my heart are poets who have been dead a hundred years.*

to all lanes—

> *I'm replying in regards to your classified in regards to obtaining a lady, who would be able to adapt to the fast lanes, speeding by in one's life span. I'm the very lady whom you are seeking . . . capable of handling ALL LANES.*

From sports lovers into everything but discus throwing—

> *I enjoy sports both as spectator and participant (golf, tennis, racquetball, roller-skating, ice-skating, hockey, bowling, football, basketball, soccer, archery, long-distance running . . .) and have a special love for fast cars.*

to the opposite—

> *I must confess I'm really not a sports fan . . . the things I've learned about sports I learned from the 'Good Doctor' column in 'Inside Sports' so I've probably never heard of you but am impressed enough with self-disciplined athletes to flatter you if you like that sort of thing.*

Those who feel they are suffering from the cheerleader syndrome—

> *Unfortunately you are my first encounter with answering a companionship ad . . . my reason for considering this source is my continuous misfor-*

tune with men. Most people assume beautiful women like myself have men at their beckon call [sic], well, I'm here to tell you that's a myth . . . men shy away from me and it certainly doesn't help matters.

and those who aren't suffering at all—

I'm sure we share a few common diversions . . . physically, I am very pretty, 5'6", and well-endowed. Thin, not skinny, and muscular to an extent . . . get in touch.

From the overly impressed—

I'm a professional person who's looking for just what you are . . . however, since I'm sending along a NUDE photo, I expect you to do the same . . . write and tell me what you expect, I'm sure I can accommodate you.

to those with reservations (to a degree)—

I'd like to talk to you and get to know you, if you're willing. But please, be yourself, don't be a phony. I don't know about you but I'm tired of people putting on airs of 'who' they are by name alone, and not what they are for the person inside them.

a few knew what to expect—

If you are interested in meeting a simpleminded, shallow, silly woman like most athletes are attracted to then don't bother reading any further; however, if you placed your ad to single out the above from those of us who don't hang out at singles bars because we don't like to be pawed, bothered, or held captive in inane conversation, read on.

OUT-OF-TOWN CONNECTION

AGGRESSIVE, brilliant attorney (34), frequent visitor [to your city], seeks intelligent, successful, funny, well-proportioned woman (25–35), for occasional clandestine meetings to discuss love, death, and other significant matters. Must appreciate good food, good sex and be willing to travel. Knowledge of computer science desired, but not required.

You would think that we women who are looking would not be interested in an affair with an out-of-towner, especially one who uses such explicit phrases as "occasional clandestine meetings" and "must appreciate . . . good sex." You are thinking incorrectly.

Today's woman is independent, liberated, and has a lot to say about "love, death, and other significant matters." In pursuit of our careers, we often don't have time for a full-time relationship, only a little time for travel here and there.

This received one of my highest responses to a male ad, which certainly proves we've come a long way.

Directly

*Okay! I'll **byte**. Your **direct access** style, however, should result in **random** replies from assorted **characters**. I'd like to check out your **file organization** and see if you possess a **higher level index**. Do you have **fixed-length** thought **processing**, or are you capable of dynamic reconfiguration? . . . It's* *very difficult to write like this—slows down my* **data transfer.** *So no more* **hashing** *around, ok? . . . I'm so glad you don't require KNOWL-EDGE of computer science . . . I don't know the first thing about those* **bit-boxes.**

I'm dying of curiosity—why, oh why, do you want a computer person? I happen to be on the staff of a trade magazine dealing with this very subject and was a programmer for five years. . . . It's really bizarre, I just want to know . . . do you do dirty things with disk drives??

Could a 5'3" blond senior systems analyst (31) meet your needs? If you can deal with the kind of woman you say you are looking for . . . call me and let's intrigue each other . . .

and indirectly—

I have my own business and have for four years. . . . I have never been married and enjoy being single . . . I like the fact that you make the most of your business trips; I love exciting relationships and make every one a learning experience . . . my younger brother is into computer graphics so I'm not totally ignorant when it comes to this science . . . call!

I am an intelligent successful salesperson who travels and am not looking for a full-time relationship . . . coincidentally one of my product lines is a computer software program. . . . You're probably asking yourself why this prize is answering this ad!? By chance.

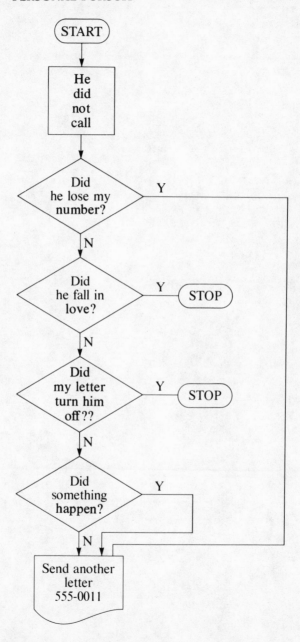

3.

PERSONAL PLUS

THE ADVANTAGES

Anonymity. Only two people are involved. If the date doesn't work out there's little or no embarrassment. And no one knows. A word to the wise: until you've had at least one date with your personal partner, don't make meeting plans at your favorite hang-out.

Ego Booster. There's nothing better for an ego than receiving fifty letters in the mail from admirers of the opposite sex trying to convince you to go out with them. After all, when's the last time you received fan mail? And admit it—you feel a sense of power reading all those letters and deciding their fate.

Time Saver. Using an ad allows you to list your requirements in a concise manner and not waste time going out with someone unsuited to you and vice versa. For example, if Mr. X placed the following ad:

I'm 29 and looking. Only young, trim, buxom and *natural* blondes need apply.

Ms. X wouldn't (or shouldn't) answer if she doesn't fit the bill.

You can even go so far as to request a resume and set up an interview:

> Good looking, rich, youthful gentleman wants to share his lovely estate home. Must be non-smoking, beautiful, and neat. Free room, free board, no strings attached. This straight, health-conscious man appreciates beauty in his surroundings and would enjoy a lovely escort. Please send detailed letter, resume, include photo and phone, for personal interview.

Money saver. Personals are a great alternative to going on welfare. Invest the $15 or $18, place an ad, and rake in the responses. If the response is anything above weird, go out and eat for free. Make a date for every other night for the rest of your life. (As for the man who places an ad, the only way you'll eat dinner for free is if you can convince a woman to cook dinner for you at her house. You can hold out for that, but it's not too likely. We all have to be careful and a woman is not going to let a stranger into her house.)

Don't forget, there's such a thing as a doggie bag, and there is no rule that you can't take bread home from a restaurant.

4.

PERSONAL GUIDANCE

RÉPONDEZ-MOI?

The purpose of this section is to help you in your effort to achieve a relationship through classified love. There are several things that you should keep in mind when deciding which ads to answer.

Be careful when you select the publication. It often dictates the type of relationship the advertiser is looking for. (See Chapter 7 for helpful descriptions of these magazines and newspapers.) Some typical examples:

SEX DIGEST:

HORNY young female desires well-endowed males for lasting action. She is 5 ft. 2 in., 125 lbs., blond hair and green eyes. All cultures enjoyed.

SWINGERS' CONTACT MAGAZINE:

CAUCASIAN COUPLE, both 32, are looking for another Caucasian couple to swing with. No pain. Send photo and address.

BOOK REVIEW PUBLICATION:

TIRED OF people who think Rimbaud is a kind of cheese? So am I, NYC writer, WM, 30, seeks woman culture maven.

Sex. It's your choice: the same, different, or both. But be sure the person you respond to shares your desires. For example, in answer to one of my ads seeking male companionship, a woman wrote:

"You can go out with me if you are gay or lesbian . . ."

She should have answered an ad such as:

GWF* (40s), 5'8", attractive, seeks good-natured outgoing GWF for possible serious relationship. Serious replies only.

Age. Again, your choice. Pick a range before you start reading—and remember that just because you are interested in a relationship with an older man or woman, the same may not be true for the advertiser. Obviously if they were interested in that type of relationship, they would advertise for it, as:

EAST SIDE professional man (55) would like relationship with somewhat younger woman with wit, curiosity, physical enthusiasm, and independence of thought. I enjoy sports, jazz, and good conversation. Photo requested.

Marital status. Important to some, not to others. Get a grip on what you are actually seeking. This may or may not be what you want:

* Gay White Female

MARRIED exec, 45, easygoing, normal, visits NY once every 1–2 mos. Seeks discreet lady for daytime meetings. Pleasant, non-tense personality more important than beauty.

Content. This is the key to picking the right person. The ad should stimulate you, intrigue you, and leave you fantasizing about the person behind it:

CARO: LA poet, 35, beautiful dinosaur who survived Ice Age, will wait as long as it takes for seething, shivering artist. We may be lost (temporarily) but hope is not.

A word of caution. Remember that while many people placing ads are sincere, many of them are out for what they can get. Do not necessarily believe ads that announce the following:

WEALTH:

MAN (54) seeks well-proportioned, attractive, romantic lady (45–52) with a net worth of $125,000, preferably Lutheran, for serious complete relationship prior to possible near-term retirement together.

PROFESSION:

ACADEMIC PHYSICIAN, 39, attractive, divorced, NYC wintering Miami, seeks very attractive intelligent woman 20–35 to join him luxury waterfront condo; marina, heated pools, sauna, tennis, et al.— weekend, month. Also seek meet same residing southern Florida. Phone/photo appreciated.

TRAVEL:

EUROPEAN BUSINESSMAN 40s going on vacation & pleasure to Aruba island for Feb. 20–28. Need attractive female for companionship & all expenses paid. Please hurry with phone #.

POSSESSIONS:

LUXURY YACHT—SWM* early 50s sks company of attractive female to live on yacht in Chesapeake area. I am cute, adorable, sexy, financially secure.

FETISHES:

HEAVY LEGS—LA Lawyer, 48, 5'11", 170, seeks WF** over 5'6" very heavy ankles & calves, slender waist and above.

You should look for originality, common interests, straightforwardness, and specifics that appeal to *you*.

HOW TO ANSWER THE AD AND HOW NOT TO

When answering an ad, remember that two hundred other people may be answering the same ad. If you are not original and don't put your best foot forward, then you are wasting your time. This person said it well:

My task here is to sell myself, to make myself wanted, needed . . .

But taking a negative point of view gets you nowhere:

I will leave it brief and to the point, realizing you have probably been bored with volumes of inquiries . . .

Neither will a typically boring response:

I'm 31, single and have a nicely decorated apartment . . .

---

* Single White Male   ** White Female

Or a lack of confidence:

> *I'm responding to your ad. I'm white, early 40s, average looking . . .*

Or being a creep:

> *If you are sincere and not just ego-tripping, call me . . .*

DON'T:	DO:
use ripped-up notebook paper (especially spiral notebook paper); it looks like you sent the other half to someone else, or worse, that you're extremely sloppy.	use stationery, personal or business, and check your spelling.
write if your handwriting is: a) illegible; or b) grossly inadequate.	use a "ghostwriter" if necessary. Use a typewriter as a last resort—handwriting is much more personal.
use legal pads. Everyone does. This shows you spent as little time as possible in preparing your answer.	use a colored envelope—it shows up in a crowd.
send a photocopy or a form letter.	send a greeting card, a picture postcard, etc. Use your imagination and be original.
write more than a page	be distinctive and straightforward
be overconfident	be confident

MAYBES

Photos. If you look like Bo Derek or Robert Redford, or if your photographer did one hell of a job airbrushing, send a photo. Otherwise, I don't suggest it.

Letterhead/Business Cards. Only if you're unattached or have an unshatterable ego should you use your letterhead or your business card when sending a response.

NOT NECESSARY

SASE (self-addressed stamped envelope). You are just wasting your money. If a person is going to answer you, he will do so, SASE or not. Let him spend 20¢; you spent 20¢ to write to him.

Newspaper articles/poetry. You can allude to it but save something for your first meeting. You'll leave the reader feeling you are overly aggressive or that your ego needs taming.

Gifts/dinner coupons/theater tickets. If someone wants to answer you, she will without this payoff. You are wasting your time and effort. She'll use the tickets and you'll never hear from her, unless you send one and keep the other! That's a great idea for a rendezvous.

20¢. Many people sent two dimes to assure a response. This showed me a lack of confidence on their part or a serious case of "manners."

BE DISCREET

For some reason, people responding have no concept of how small the world is. I knew many of the men and women who responded to me—not all personally, but there was a connection in one way or another.

I was amazed at the lack of discretion, especially on the part of the married or coupled men and women who responded. Many of the people used business stationery, wrote to me of their past, present, and (imagined) future. Mate put-downs were prevalent, statements of boredom overwhelming, and sexual dissatisfaction predominant. If I were into blackmail, I'd be a rich woman.

CONTACT ARRANGEMENTS

Part of your letter should incorporate how the person you are writing can get in touch with you. Give your phone number or address and that's it. Other instructions leave people feeling suspicious—for example, pre-set times, private post office boxes, meetings at shopping malls. Do not ask them to place a personal ad in the newspaper or in a magazine; this is very costly. Why should they when they have so many other letters to consider?

COMPOSITION 101

To be successful at classified love and ensure a high response, there are several things to keep in mind when composing your ad: sex, age, personal status, and some type of angle.

Although most personal ads begin with male or female, it's not necessary to start that way. I say keep 'em guessing.

SIREN seriously suggests sensational soiree with suave stud spending substantial cents for superbly satisfying sortie. Those with lisps need not apply.

ELIZABETH TAYLOR LOOK-ALIKE needs help. New to this area; have been told 23 times by men and women that I look like Liz. Isn't there any man that isn't intimidated by a look-alike. I like intelligent, humorous, financially secure male, 40.

NEED A TAX SHELTER? I may be it. Pretty, trim landlady (youthful 38) seeks good humor man. A warm heart and a cold drink wait.

HEAD ON RIGHT. Lights green. Mind swift. Un-
afraid of feelings. Professional (mid-40s). Looking
for female counterpart.

Decide how important age is. If you're sixteen, you
may decide to leave that out or lie. If you're of an ac-
ceptable age (I make no judgment), then by all means
state it, but don't get too far off.

Then decide what age group you are trying to attract. If you have no preference either way, there is no
need to set guidelines; but if you do have guidelines,
do not advertise "into roller-skating, skinny-dipping,
and drugs" if you're looking for someone mature.

If you have a set range in mind, don't be afraid to
put it into print—all ages answer anyway.

Sometimes your personal status makes no difference, but depending on the types of people you wish to
attract, you may want to mention that you're married
and your wife or husband lives twelve hundred miles
away. However, this can backfire. If you're a male, saying you're divorced gets sympathy, as does being a
widower, but saying you're married gets laughs. (I
must point out, however, that my "MARRIED
WOMAN" ad had the highest response of all my ads
from those seeking "no strings" fun.)

Are you out for "sex for sex's sake"? Do you want
another divorced person with children in your same
situation? Do you want a serious relationship or are you
interested in a one-night stand? Do you need someone
into airplanes, helicopters, and wings, or are you a
ground sports enthusiast? These things are important if
you want your ad to work for you. Once you've decided
the angle and the subjects you wish to pursue, the ad
will be a lot easier to write. Ads with no angle get very
little response—they're boring.

MALE (29) wishing to meet female (22–30), slim, for sincere relationship.

MALE (26) would like to meet a nice lady for fun and good times.

ATTRACTIVE FEMALE (22) seeks tall, handsome, never married professional (22–29). Photo appreciated.

QUIET, SENSITIVE SINGLE MAN (30s), looking for genuine friendship or lasting relationship with opposite sex.

SINGLE FEMALE seeks single male (over 33), for serious stable relationship.

THE AD

Now that you've got everything outlined, you know what you're looking for, and you've narrowed down the age group and status, go ahead and write the ad. But keep the following in mind:

Key words or phrases. The key to placing personal ads is, of course, the ad itself. What I found in virtually every case was that the more humorous, original, or strange the ad, the higher the response. Key words chosen from the ad were used in almost every response, even if it wasn't the key phrase or word *I* had in mind when *I* wrote the ad.

For example, in "MARRIED WOMAN" (p. XV) "discreet" was the word respondents really got off on:

> *I am an unattached lawyer who is the absolute soul of* **discretion** *. . . Strings? I have none.*

I am single and I own my own house in a very **discreet** *part of the city.*

You asked for **discreet**—*let's try this: if interested pick weekday from week of July 21 through July 28; then go to Jones Mall, wait on a mall bench in front of Jack's Sporting Goods between 12:00 and 12:30. Have* **Time** *magazine visible so I'll know it's you. Pick day most convenient. I'll check each day. Code words, me: "Is that this week's* **Time**?" *You: "Are you Dick?"*

In "STEPPED-ON GIRL" (p. 27) "vegetables" got the most notoriety although "stepped-on" and "special" stuck in some people's mind:

I choose to write to you precisely because of that word **vegetables.** *If you do not want any vegetables, you must not be, I assume, a vegetable yourself; therefore, I wrote to you.*

Someone **special** *should be attractive but not fat.*

In "WOMAN (27) SEEKS ROOMMATE" (p. 73) "boring" brought out the best in people:

You are a woman of few words . . . recently divorced, short marriage . . . I kept the bed and I too am **bored.**

And lastly, "FEMALE SEEKS SUPERIOR" (p. 32) had every man denying he was either "conceited" or "obnoxious," and "object matrimony" deterred no one:

I am reasonably sure I meet most of your criteria and I am absolutely certain I meet one of them . . . obviously **conceited** *(what Harvard Law School graduate isn't?), but I'm not* **obnoxious.**

*Saw your ad. I am not obviously **conceited;** however, subtly so.*

Ads that are too specific (religion, nationality, astrology) receive the fewest responses. Of course, ads offering "no strings" relationships, such as "HOT POTATO" (p. 65) and "MARRIED WOMAN" (p. XV), receive the most. Surprisingly, "PROSPEROUS FEMALE" (p. 44) received a very high response, a point well taken for older women.

Using key phrases keeps the reader guessing the true meaning of your ad. This is a point in your favor:

. . . Would like to meet attractive, slender, educated, traditional woman (45–50), *for the usual reasons*.

I venture to say this man received tons of letters asking "what are the usual reasons?"

Gimmick. All of the following had some type of angle:

MILLIONAIRESS WANTED—young, brilliant, beautiful, accomplished, passionate, aesthetic—for encounter with the most fascinating romantic man you're likely to meet on this planet.

SWM—trim, 38, professional, will exchange French lessons and/or ballroom dancing (including hustle) for any other fun skill taught by neat female under 42.

HAVING SPENT an inordinate amount of time sentiently searching for security, stability, and THE AMERICAN DREAM, I am now gloriously approaching boredom, slowed only by the products of my search. May I borrow the station wagon to go to the dump? Shall we discuss it over lunch?

MALE (29) seeks mature or immature female for intimate one-night stands or more. Photo appreciated.

Humor is necessary to attract likable human beings with some personality:

WANTED: ATTRACTIVE FEMALE interested in watching slides of Poland.

PROFESSIONAL SINGLE MALE (33), flunked Disco and Bars 101, would like to meet a lady (28–48) who likes water sports, movies, and the fun things in life. Photo please.

Pretty, athletic, sentimental, emotional, home-loving businesswoman, two part-time children, one dog who is under psychiatric care, seeks educated man (between 38 and death).

Handsome, blue-eyed blond male, Yale class of '92, seeks female companion with similar long-range goals. Must be of good stock, but *nouveau riche* considered.

Originality is useful when sorting through responses. If you are original, so will your respondents be—like gets like:

IT'S UNFASHIONABLE at my age (36) to be still examining the mysteries of life seeking enlightenment. But—sigh—you gotta follow your heart. Besides, we're all bozos on this bus. Still, an attractive woman of kindred spirit to share the journey with might be nice. Must have own clown shoes.

UP FOR ADOPTION: Single mother (34), two rug-rats. Good cook: does not do windows. Unconventional. Adventurous. Funny, with serious streak. Excellent vices.

THIS ONE'S FOR YOU wherever you are. He's 29, attractive, intelligent, honest, romantic, athletic, poetic, sensitive, understanding, conscientious, diligent, witty, fun to be with, persevering, caring, sharing, reliable, patient, indefatigable, magical, scintillating, enigmatic & stubborn! Hey nobody's perfect. Thank God, he's real. He's alive & he's single but best of all, he's me.

DIRTY OLD Elizabethan DWMCP—wants a bright and attractive wench to age 45 for fun, fights, and frolic. "If a wedding ring you need, in the other ads do read" . . . But . . . if you want good times, lots of TLC, and mayhap a modicum of involvement, then join me in a wee dram or two whilst we discuss on it.

ANN ARBOR AREA. Attractive woman seeking Prince Charming trapped in froggy skin of inappropriate marriage, warm sharing friendship to make both of us human again.

Use a magazine box number. As I mentioned before, personal post office boxes give people the wrong impression. And telephone numbers are a waste of time. One year and over 20,000 phone calls later, I realized I would never have the time or the ability to sort through all these messages. Although the first few tapes were quite amusing (and quite sordid), there was no way to determine the qualifications of a candidate from only a message on an answering machine. Although I have talked with men who put their phone numbers in the personals with better results, I don't recommend it to your normal, all marbles present, searching female.

WHERE TO PLACE AN AD

Depending on the type of person and the type of relationship you are seeking, here are the types of publications that print personal ads starting with the largest coverage to the most select.

Sex periodicals (commonly known in my circle as "newsstand porn"). Many of today's sex magazines, available from drugstores to supermarkets, are now devoting a section to personal ads. Place your ad here only if you have an interest in other than a sincere relationship and have a good doctor. Be sure to include city and state.

Good for you if you're looking for raw sex relationships in your own and others' cities.

Swinging mags. Every day a new "swinging" publication comes out. You can place not only your personal ad but a personal photo as well, usually in any pose you desire. They are cover-to-cover ads with not much in between (recently I saw one with over six thousand ads for one month) and divided into geographical areas.

A true waste of time and money unless you're into that sort of thing. But don't expect too many responses when another 5,999 people are advertising for the same thing.

Newspapers. You can pick up most any large newspaper in this country and find columns of personal ads.

The coverage is great, but you really have no indication as to the type of person who will answer you—from Joe Schmo down the street to your favorite physician.

Good only if you own a private post office box.

Singles publications. Many cities are coming out with magazines for singles. Here you are on the same level with other singles in your area, and at least you've narrowed the field to others in the same boat and same city.

Good for a chance to have a sincere relationship.

City magazines. Most major cities in the country are now publishing a good-sized magazine of local happenings. Most of these magazines have personal columns in the classified ad section. If not, start one—I don't think they'd refuse cash in hand. And think of the response you'll get if yours is the only ad. Usually these magazines attract a more cultural and more professional group.

Good for the woman whose mother wants her to marry a doctor or lawyer.

Special interest publications. Here you have narrowed down your coverage even more. Pick the subjects you're most interested in and I guarantee that you can find a magazine on the market that has to do with that hobby or pastime. For instance, if you're heavily into classical music and longhairs, advertise in a music digest of some sort. The classier the subject the classier the answers.

Good for snobs.

INTERPRETATION 101

There are certain things you should be cautious about when reading through the responses to your personal ad.

Private phone numbers. This usually announces that
the person answering is either married or attached in
some way—not necessarily a good one. Anyone who
has a private phone number has it for a reason. If you
can't help but answer because the letter is so original,
expect the unexpected.

Personal post office boxes. Be very cautious of people
with their own private post office box as opposed to a
box number at the magazine or newspaper. They are
either married or extremely paranoid. This is a serious
game for many people and only a game; therefore, there
is doubtful possibility for a long-term relationship.

Strange addresses. Many people will give you mailing addresses of their friends, hotels, bars, etc., instead
of their own. What is the necessity for these complicated
arrangements?

Corporate stationery. Sometimes people aren't what
they appear to be. A disappointing but humorous response came on letterhead from one of the largest tire
and rubber companies in America. The stationery was
headed "Office of the President." You can imagine my
surprise and delight. What a catch, not to mention free
tires for the rest of my adult life.

But as I read his letter, something was amiss

*. . . You are just what I've been looking for. I am
married and have three children but I surely do
need some outside diversion and you stated in
your ad "no monetary obligation" and at times
with my family I'm running close . . .*

I always thought the guys at the top made a lot of
money. They certainly work long hours

*. . . please excuse my sloppy handwriting but it is
midnight and I started my day at 8 a.m. . .*

as I read further, I realized things in the rubber industry must really be tough

> . . . *please don't think I am a welfare case* . . .
> *but* . . . *I have a steady part time job from 6 –10*
> *every evening Monday through Friday* . . .

however, my sympathy diminished when I read

> . . . *I have a carpet cleaning job here tonight and*
> *when I saw the magazine I picked it up to read.*
> *Thus explaining the headings on the envelope and*
> *paper. I'll bet you thought some big executive was*
> *writing you! Ha Ha!*

No name. This isn't frequent. Surprisingly, most people will give their first and last name; so why bother with someone who doesn't?

People who send suggestive photos. Obviously anyone who would send a personal photo of himself in his underwear, or in no underwear, is strange.

Professionals. Many people claim to be doctors, attorneys, writers, artists, and more. Be wary of these people, especially those claiming to be doctors. It may be a con. Just because they write to you on medical supply house notepaper doesn't deem them doctors. They know that with a professional occupation, they are assumed to be pillars of the community with an aura of money and prestige. This isn't necessarily so.

Offers of gifts and travel. One has to wonder why anyone would offer gifts, money, trips, and God knows what to someone he or she barely even knows. Be cautious of these people; they are probably married and looking for something from you other than the normal relationship.

Threesomes. I don't think I need say anything about this except that it isn't your normal sincere run-of-the-mill relationship.

Inmates. It is very nice to write to prison inmates so that they have pen pals, but I have heard many stories of unsuspecting females who are easily swayed and end up sending money and presents to these men. Keep your sympathy in check.

Blitzers. It is the habit of a very few to blitz the ads, that is, to answer every personal ad no matter who's behind it. The blitzer sends a photocopy of an original letter and signs it personally—sometimes. But beware, blitzers may handwrite the same letter five times a month, month after month after month.

The blitzer might respond to all of the following in the same month:

BLACK FEMALE (40s), petite and shy, seeks companionship.

EAST SIDE WOMAN (early 20s), Caucasian, seeks sincere relationship with blue-collar worker.

Pretty, petite, aggressive medical professional lady wants to meet doctor, dentist, or vet.

Telltale signs of blitzing that stick out like a sore thumb are photocopies, an original letter copied verbatim (you can tell because the response does not address itself to your ad), and a business card with no letter.

One foolproof method of eliminating these pests is to place more than one ad. If a person answers both, you know it wasn't just your ad that appealed to him or her. Another solution is to compare notes with your friends who are advertising at the same time. Some people will go as far as to respond to eight to ten ads in one month, with a different letter to each, varying age, occupation, and even marital status.

Sympathy seekers. Leave your bleeding heart where it belongs.

Out-of-towners. People from out of town will write that they will be in your city three or four times a month and would like to have a relationship. Who wouldn't? I question their motives. Of course, on the other hand, you may enjoy that type of thing.

Keep the following in mind when trying to select a response:

Handwriting. Handwriting tells a great deal about the person—we all know that. You can usually tell if a person is neat, together, aggressive, and so forth.

Grammar, spelling, and all that goes with it. Grammar and especially spelling tell a lot about a person. Although I know very intelligent people who can't spell, you have to draw the line somewhere. You must decide for yourself exactly what your requirements are.

Stationery. Again, many people use legal paper, notebook paper, scratch pads, you name it. This tells a lot about the person—how much time he put into his response, how sincere she is, and more.

Content. This is most important; it tells you more about a person than anything else. There are pluses and minuses.

PLUSES	MINUSES
Is he sincere?	Is he ego-tripping?
Is he original?	Is he looking for sympathy?

Does he have a sense of humor?	Has he made too many promises?
Is he truthful?	Is the letter very very short—three words or less?
Is he realistic?	Is the letter very very long—more than a page?
Is he crazy?	Is he crazy?

THE RENDEZVOUS

While I think classified love is a great substitute for the bar scene, fix-ups and blind dates, people are still leery of personal ads and the people they breed. For them I have several options that are not only security inclined but enjoyable.

The go-between. Many people are success oriented. Their ads list not only qualifications but desired results. Most of the men and women who would use a go-between such as a lawyer, a family friend, or a private detective are interested in nothing less than marriage. Be prepared to go through a thorough investigative probing:

> Aristocratic woman of means seeks male of same status in life for relationship leading to something permanent . . . marriage. Send resume and qualifications for possible interview with my attorney.

I know of two situations where this type of ad has produced wondrous results. Both couples are now happily married. Or were.

Dinner party (safety in numbers). In the _____ 1981 issue of *Cosmopolitan*, Gini Graham Scott wrote about her experiences after she and two friends advertised for three men for a dinner party:

> Attention: Handsome, successful, professional men . . . 3 attractive ladies would like to invite you to dinner . . . we cook the dinner, you bring the wine . . . for an invitation, write.

Since then, this kind of ad has popped up all over the country. If her article is any indication, it's a great idea.

Public makes perfect. Meeting in a public place is always a good safeguard against ill happenings. If you are really nervous, have a friend hidden in the wings who with the least provocation will leap to your rescue (from harm or just boredom).

The Bobbsey Twin syndrome. Most of us have that one special friend from whom we are inseparable (I have ten of them). There is nothing wrong with showing up for your date with your best friend in tow. You never know—he or she could be a better match for your personals partner than you are.

Group function. I have never tried this, but I can imagine a fine time. Invite the entire personals column (one month or more) to a party. Instead of a name, each person wears his or her box number and a cut-out copy of the ad on a tag. Stand back and watch.

Question/Answer Guide or Everything You Always Wanted to Know About Personal Ads but Were Too Embarrassed to Ask

While researching this book, I was deluged with inquiries from friend and foe. Not until these questions started to pop up did I realize how little people knew about the personal ads that appear in our major

magazines and newspapers. Most people were sure
these ads were listed for entertainment purposes only
and were made up by the publication's staff. And even
some people who participated weren't exactly sure
what went on.

By answering these questions I hope to clear up any
doubts and confusion.

Will I be killed?
I've never met anyone who was.

Do more men answer or more women?
Although women generally place more ads than
men, men's responses outnumber women's thirty
to one.

Are the ads for real? Are these people normal and sincere?
Most of the people behind the ads are normal and
the people who respond are especially sincere. Remember, although the ads sound off-the-wall, these
people are competing to be noticed. I would caution, though, against responding to someone advertising for a person into diapers.

Do some people respond to more than one ad at a time? Should they?
I don't suggest it; frequently I have four or five ads
in one magazine for an assortment of people who
are totally different (age, status, etc.). Many people
answered all of them. I ignored these people.

Are people what they describe themselves to be or are they generally ugly?
Men claim the women are *never* what they say they
are—physically so; women say the men usually
have acne.

Can I write off the expense of the ad (or the meal)—if it doesn't pan out—as a casualty loss?
Check with your accountant.

What's the average number of ads in a major city magazine?
Anywhere from 1 to 150.

Will my name be kept confidential when I place an ad?
Usually. But everyone has a price.

Will the magazine read my mail?
You never know. If they open the letter, they'll keep it. A good way to check is to mail a letter to yourself. Don't make it too long.

Should I use a magazine box number?
This is usually the easiest way. Personal P.O. boxes lead the reader to believe you make a habit of this sort of thing.

Are the box numbers real or made up?
They are made up; the number is used to identify the advertiser. Letters are then kept numerically filed until mailed.

How often will mail be forwarded? and for how long?
Usually once a week. Most magazines will let you pick the letters up on a daily basis if you have schpilkes (high anxiety). Letters are usually forwarded for one year from the date of the ad.

Are there free places to advertise?
Most cities do have tabloids and underground newspapers that take free ads.

What's the average cost of those that charge?
About $1 per word and a charge for a box number. This varies according to publication.

Will the magazine edit my ad?

If you're lucky—but not too often unless it's suggestive beyond repair . . . then they may refuse to print it.

How soon after I answer an ad will the advertiser get my letter?

If the letters are forwarded weekly you can expect as much as a 10–14-day lapse. If after six months you still haven't heard anything, chances are you won't. Try again.

How long do I have to respond to an ad?

Usually up to one year. Most magazines list instructions. Be first, be last; you'll have a better chance. If you wait a few months the letters will have stopped coming in and you'll be alone in the crowd.

If I put several responses in an envelope, will the magazine sort and forward them?

Yes, and it's a good way to save postage.

Should I place more than one ad?

This is a good idea. Get together with friends and write several ads. This will flush out the regulars and leave you with the cream of the crop—not yet homogenized.

Should I request a photo?

A picture definitely helps when trying to sort out which responses to pursue but it also inhibits potential respondents. Remember, you'll get pictures whether you request them or not . . . *all kinds*.

Should I put my phone number or address in the ad?

If you do, expect to be plagued by unending phone calls and nighttime visitors. Most callers think a minimum of 95 rings is necessary before they're sure no one is home.

Will the magazine space my ad according to my instructions?

The magazines I dealt with did not want to do this but could be influenced if I was willing to pay an extra charge.

Should I respond to more than one ad?

There is no reason not to if you are interested in the people as they represented themselves in their ads. To blitz the ads will cause you problems in the long run.

If I respond to more than one, should I send a typed form letter or an original?

Never send a copy or a form letter. The advertiser will think you have answered the world.

If I respond to more than one ad, should I change my name each time?

Only if you're planning to skip town.

Should I answer an ad if I don't meet the qualifications listed?

Why waste your time? Chances are unless you write an extraordinary response, you'll never hear from the advertiser.

Is it possible to remain anonymous in responding to an ad?

Yes; but don't expect a phone call or letter in return. Why should they call you when everyone else signs a first name (and usually last name, measurements, address, date of birth, astrological sign, etc.)?

How many responses to my ad should I expect to get?

My average was very high but I spent an extraordinary amount of time composing my ads. A good ad which is humorous as well as original should net you anywhere from 20 to 150 responses. The fewer the ads in the publication, the higher the response (unless people don't know they're there).

How many dates should I expect to reap from my responses?

Some people go out with every response. Others are choosy and pick three or four of the best and throw away the rest. Your best bet is to be discriminating.

Should I check out the respondent? Should I verify the qualifications as listed in the response?

Evil minds work in evil ways. If it doesn't cause much hardship (don't hire a private detective), find out as much about the person as you can before contacting him.

Should I run a D & B?

It's costly, but what the hey?

Is handwriting important?

Well, it does give you insight. Someone who writes unintelligibly probably speaks unintelligibly.

Should I call or write?

You may not have a choice. But if you have the option, by all means call—it's quicker, among other obvious reasons.

Should I make a date during the first conversation?

If the answers to your first five questions please you, go right ahead.

Should I discuss sex?

That depends on yours (sex, that is), what the ad read, and what the response read.

What time period is too late to answer a response?
None. But if you wait five years you run the risk of being labeled a procrastinator.

Do responses expire?
Watch the obituaries.

Is it good practice to meet at a place of mutual choice or at home?
Never meet at home. If you're a woman, pick a public place and let your friends know where you're going (or bring them with you for that matter). Men shouldn't request to meet a woman at home—again there's that "label" aspect to consider (pervert, weirdo, kinkette, etc.).

Who should pay?
Tricky! That should be discussed up front. If a woman places the ad and calls a respondent for a date, she's expected to pay just like that. Don't forget—you're liberated.

Should I bring my pet on the first date?
Only if it's a Doberman.

Will I get sued for date-imony?
Call Marvin Mitchelson.

Can I expect to be engaged by the end of the evening?
How fast do you run the quarter mile?

When should I get discouraged?
Never.

5.

PERSONAL PRIDE

GOOD READS

For your entertainment, I have collected ads from virtually every publication all over the United States. From religious journals to cooking guides, from city magazines to those not-so-hard-to-find sleaze papers, personal ads abound. If you want to use some of their ideas to help you write your own ad, help yourself.

I found the following ads to be out of the ordinary. They are certainly not typical, although not uncommon.

GODFATHER type (50s) offers struggling young woman (20–40) aid and advice in non–interfering pragmatic exchange.

WIDOW, early 50s, $100,000 net worth, seeks widower with same. Object: retire together.

115

ADVENTUROUS—bisexual male seeks female of like personality for mutual experiences and possible marriage.

TIRED OF DIETING to please everyone? This hairy-chested SWM prefers the before pictures of diet advertisements. Seeks SWF under 31.

ATTRACTIVE, feminine, queen-sized lady seeks sensitive, unattached male.

KNOWLEDGEABLE in the art of fasting? Woman who needs to fast desires to spend time with man over 35 years of age.

SWM, 36, attractive, balding, 5'11", educated, government manager, seeks continuing date or relationship to explore local Swingers clubs and groups.

SWINGING MALE, 33, looking for *two* attractive women (18–21) as companions on 30-day Atlantic cruise.

LOVELY delightful Jewish woman in late 30s looking for a knight on a white stallion. No head games allowed.

DOG, 4, tired of seeing owner, 26, pretty, college-educated East Sider, with same old people. Looking for single male.

Damsel in distress, 27, blond, professional, attractive, multifaceted, awaits established knight with same attributes for continuing relationship. Steed need not apply.

HANDSOME, wealthy, mature gentleman (race-horse owner/breeder) seeks companion 18–28 yrs. old. Will furnish new car, nice home, fun, excitement, travel; will support education or career. Send photo and resume.

BLACK MALE 27 needs a female partner 18–50 for fun times at Plato's Retreat. Send phone.

WHITE MARRIED FEMALE seeks man for discreet erotic encounters.

YOUTHFUL MIDDLE-AGED business lady. Husband with tired blood—would like to meet woman in similar circumstances. Strict confidence.

WHITE MALE 39, professional, very attractive, intelligent, warm, sensual seeks enchantress, elegantly impassioned in her world of black silks and satins.

ATTRACTIVE PROFESSIONAL SJF 32 seeks intelligent sincere SANE single white male 30–45.

THREE'S COMPANY—attractive white couple 28, 30 seeks attractive slender white female for sensual evenings. Shy, eager, honest, and discreet. Send photo and phone . . . serious replies only.

ATTRACTIVE SENSUOUS couple wish friendship and dates with attractive gal. Will visit New York the 14–20 and periodically thereafter.

TAKE TIME OUT DURING FOOTBALL SEASON. *You won't be disappointed.* Attractive, vivacious, professional female eager to meet single Jewish men (28–36), with same qualities.

JEWISH BUSINESS EXEC (29), tired of giving and not receiving; of being "just friends" and "brother type". Would like to meet Jewish lady (26–35), who is willing to give and receive T.L.C. *Took time out from football; very disappointing.* Kvetches need not respond.

DON RICKLES THINK-ALIKE, insincere (40), seeks like-minded woman for part-time, no promises fun.

OMAR SHARIF LOOK-ALIKE, successful financial executive, seeks very good-looking, sophisticated lady 24–32.

LESLIE CARON LOOK-ALIKE: WJF early 30s, 5'1", attr, slim, bright exec w/2 daughters & interests of music, theatre, skiing, photog, sailing, dancing, sks bright WM non-smoker to share interests & exp life. Phone pls.

LON CHANEY LOOK-ALIKE (just joking; but we all can't be as handsome as some people in these ads), 33, slim, creative, impossibly elegant, with martini-dry sense of humor, sks sultry, naughty, slim SWF for erotic encounters that will leave you breathless with laughter. Photo/phone, if you please.

I NEVER THOUGHT MY HUSBAND would leave me for a younger woman. He didn't; she was older. Anyone anxious to make it all better 'permanently,' please answer. Photos appreciated.

PLATO, MOZART, WODEHOUSE are fine company but one can't dine with them. Presentable, generally happy middle-aged Chicago lady seeks pleasant companions for dutch-treat excursions restaurants, clubs, theaters, galleries etc. Age, sex immaterial. Romance (hetero) not 'hors discours' but tertiary.

WANTED: 4 postmenopausal frogs (transformable to princes) not threatened by, but equal to, 4 exceptional, secure, mature attractive DJW for 1981 serious/sincere twosomes.

4 SWF travel agents seek
A. SWM British blonde blue-eyed 22–35
B. SBM Prof financially secure 40–45
C. SWM wealthy, witty, wise 35–50
D. SWM Italian Eng. speaking 25–35
phone/photo if poss. indicate a, b, c, d

LA MAN. Attractive, sense of humor, sensitive, seeks same-time next-week relationship with companionable, comely woman.

CONSERVATIVE, healthy, divorced corporate career lady of forty with a middle-of-the-road weight problem and family grown, desires to return to family life—possibly with a single male parent in forties needing companionship on the domestic scene.

DWF age 50—Unconventional (to some), conventional (to others). Sophisticated, naive. Witty, open, liberated; dull, secretive, traditional. Modest, arrogant. Ambitious, accepting; demanding, content.

Seeking man who appreciates life's contradictions and absurdities for caring, sharing, companionship.

WILD WOMAN WANTED: Financially secure, romantic, gd-looking exec 33, WM throws wild sumptuous gourmet parties in his E. Side townhse—no holds barred sks attrac, loving lady to join in.

GENTLEMAN (58), 5'11", 160 lbs., modest income, interests include civil liberties, ecology, para-psychology, politics, etc. Seeks marriage contract with feminist. Respondent should be supportive of ERA and related issues. Sees society as a male-dominated institution in which she refuses to take the traditional subservient role. Will not compromise her social, political, economic, or religious ethics to curry favor with any male regardless of his position in her life. Women involved should be non-smoker, in reasonably good health; age, physical appearance, social, political, economic, or religious background irrelevant.

ATTR SWM, 35, seeks liberated, vigorous attr SWF who prefers celibacy to conformity.

TRAVEL!??—MWM, 38, seeks discreet, attractive WF, 20–35 to share experiences two or three times a year. Travel to exotic places, live and dine together in splendor. I work; you swim, lounge, and sightsee. We do the evenings together. No commitments.

BIRTHDAY GIRL—active SWF 26, seeks tall, handsome, romantic, athletic, professional SWM,

27–35, who enjoys spending money on frivolous cards, flowers, etc., besides dinners, dancing, theater, and crazy escapades, for fun, friendship. Photos, white corvettes helpful.

SM—SEEKS F who's pleasant, warm, bright, quick-witted, knowledgeable about various things, cultured, sense of humor (not corn), good taste, traveled abroad, good job; likes classical music, concerts, ballet, art, good movies, walking, biking, jogging, cooking, eating (but doesn't show it); 41–52, 5'9", 140 lbs., reasonably attractive; small bust, shapely rear; non-smoker, no children, no pets.

ARE YOU A TALL, handsome, successful, Caucasian Prince (32–39) with rescue fantasies? Attractive, intelligent, Cinderella (with size 7½ slippers) is waiting to be carried away.

LOST: Female, short, brown eyes, distant, crooked teeth, small feet, heartbreaker. Missing 9½ weeks. If found, please reply to Box __.

MULTIFACETED MATURE midwestern male medic, moderately moral, seeks sympathetic, sensitive but saucy spouseless soulmate to complete complementary creativity circle.

ATTRACTIVE GENTLEMAN FARMER (mid-20s) desires attractive females to share expenses, household chores, and supportive emotional commitment.

ATTRACTIVE MALE Caucasian, professional (32), seeks female counterpart for best friend/lover. You wouldn't believe I stay home on Saturday nights! Or would you? Please write. Odds are, YOU will not meet me otherwise.

HAPPINESS INCLUDES splendid Saturday brunch with soul-satisfying, flowing conversation plus a ramble through the Strand seeking (in my case) Rackhams, Victorian gothics. Add some chamber music—Brahms, Faure, Mozart. . . . Am DJF, 36, slimly 'Renoiresque' personnel manager/opera singer (Juilliard). Seeking civilized coexplorer of above amenities, extensively involved with the arts. Prefer single, 36–40ish, tweeds, wit, urbanity, erudition, gregariousness, touch of romanticism. Snobs welcome.

STIMULATING, ultrasymmetrical, discerning, independent NYC woman seeks quiet, serious, egregious man, 40+, with paradoxes. Aware of his androgynous nature, intense, uninhibited, ragged, enthusiastic, he oozes 'self,' has style, and wants the splendor of intimacy and mutual supportiveness. His slippers await.

A COMPLIANT, well-educ, vy attr, masc, SWM, 30s, sks SLIM, beautiful F, who hates housework, laundry, errands, shining shoes & boots.

BOXING FANTASY: Attra WM, 32, sks attra female to share my fantasy. We're boxers. I'm out. You try to revive me. First a kiss . . . Photo name and number. NO PROS.

FOOT/SHOE FETISHIST: BWM, easy to talk to, would like to hear from those turned on by feet and

shoes. I'm into brown penny loafers, old army ox-
fords w/loosened laces, and women's slip-on pumps.
I like kicking off shoes, dangling them, and playing
footsies.

AAA man seeks AAA woman: Able, accomplished,
accountable, active, adventurous, alive, assisting, attractive man, 42, aims to amplify and augment life by
allying with an affable, appealing, adorable woman,
about 35. Adventurous? Explore the alphabet with
me.

AN AD in the Voice was once placed,
By a SWF, cute, funny & chaste.
The SWM who then picked her
To send his phone number & picture
Found out his time wasn't a waste.

6.

PERSONALLY SPEAKING

ABBREVIATIONS

In most magazines and newspapers abbreviations are commonly used in the ad itself to convey marital status, race, religion, and so on. Abbreviations are also used to save money.

Feel free to make up your own abbreviations as long as your ad can be readily deciphered. For instance this man certainly cut down on the rate of illiterate responses:

ATTR affec SJM 34 510 170 v shp & v sensuous sks uninhi BF for pleas times day or eve. Bi OK. Have car & apt.

or, a guy who's original (although his shoe size, blood pressure, and cigarette brand don't do anything for me):

SWM, 31, BA, 130/80, J&B, 11-D, BLT, LSMFT.
SWF (PIX).

These are the universally accepted abbreviations
you'll find in most popular magazines:

M—married   M—male
S—single   F—female
D—divorced   YO—years old
G—gay   P/P—photo/phone
Bi—bisexual   PIX—send photo
W—white   SASE—self-addressed stamped
B—black   envelope
J—Jewish   ISO—in search of

Marital status and/or sexual preference is usually
listed first, race second, and sex last when describing
yourself:

SWF—single white female
GBM—gay black male
DJF—divorced Jewish female

There is a popular new abbreviation that was coined by
the United States Census Bureau:

POSSLQ ('pos-el-kyu) (n.) people of opposite sex
sharing living quarters.

BUZZ WORDS AND PHRASES

In reading the personals, you'll come across the
same words and phrases used time and time again. To
assist you at creating an ad that suits your needs, I have
listed these commonly used words and phrases, divid-
ing them into interesting categories.

After choosing your category, feel free to group the phrases into an ad that complements both you and your desires. For example, if you want a physical relationship, choose a phrase from the sexual or no strings category and add other key phrases or words to help you compose your ad. It may read something like this:

Hedonistic DWF (36) seeks discreet playmate for horizontal frolicking and whatever develops—NO KINKS. Box _____.

That's a no strings ad if I ever saw one. Now go ahead. But remember, *be honest* or you'll be sorely disappointed.

WHO IS SOUGHT:
    counterpart
    kindred spirit
    POSSLQ
    same
    playmate

WHAT IS SOUGHT:

NORMAL RELATIONSHIP

    for companionship
    for cerebral sharing
    for caring and sharing
    for a sincere relationship
    for a lasting relationship
    for a long-term relationship
    for a permanent relationship
    for a meaningful relationship
    for a possible lasting relationship
    for a possible serious relationship
    for a mutually satisfying relationship

ROMANTIC RELATIONSHIP

candlelight dinner
romantic dinner
romantic interlude
romantic at heart
let's plan our escape

MARRIAGE

marriage-minded
never married
entrapment

NO STRINGS RELATIONSHIP

for whatever develops
for a one-night-stand
for a *no strings* relationship
in strict confidence

SEXUAL RELATIONSHIP

horizontal frolicking
life in the fast lane
no kinks
uninhibited
well-proportioned

ADULTERY

daytime dalliance
afternoon delight
afternoon encounter
adventurous

ONE-SIDED ADULTERY

affluent
has assets
financially secure

WHY THEY'RE SOUGHT:
> a heart in the right place
> into the good life
> with _____ outlook on life
> for sharing the finer things in life
> varied interests
> similar qualities
> willing to give and receive TLC

GLOSSARY

adventurous /ad 'vench (e) res/ (adj.) one who can experience infidelity without guilt

affectionate /a 'fek sh(e) net/ (adj.) will hold any part of another person's anatomy on request

aggressive /a 'gres iv/ (adj.) a submissive in wolf's clothing

assertive /a 'sert iv/ (adj.) has mouth measurements of four by four

cerebral sharing /'ee es pee/ (n.) intellectual sparring with woman on top

classy /'klas e/ (adj.) knows birthdates of Calvin Klein and Jackie O

creative /kre 'at iv/ (adj.) can do amazing things with whipped cream

cultured /'kel cherd/ (adj.) into yogurt

discreet /dis 'kret/ (adj.) 1. fuel no hardship; let's meet out of state; 2. the most misspelled word in the English language

educated /'em bee ay/ (adj.) sixth grade just isn't enough

erotic /i 'rat ik/ (adj.) a person who likes his leather feathered

fast lane /'ko kan/ (n.) sex, drugs, and rock & roll

for whatever develops /'drem on/ (adv.) from sex on up

hedonistic /hed n 'is tik/ (adj.) into pleasure; the "try anything" type

high spirited /'tu flot/ (adj.) a mainliner

idealistic /i de e 'lis tik/ (adj.) fool enough to fall in love with you

intellectual /'dep shit/ (adj.) truly wants you for your mind and your body

intimate /'int e mat/ (adj.) the adult version of playing doctor; "I'll show you mine if you show me yours"

ivy leaguer /'prep ee/ (n.) a person with a relative named Muffy

jock /'jak/ (n.) a strap of a man

kindred spirit /'kin dred 'spir et/ (n.) one who is looking for the other pea

liberated /'lib e ratd/ (adj.) no hang-ups; beware—could mean "let's go dutch"

marriage-minded /'sik/ (adj.) marriage-minded but not marriage-oriented

no kinks /un kin 'kee/ (n.) leave your rubber hose at home

non-smoker/drinker /pyur/ (n.) health fanatic; clean teeth, clean lungs, clean mind, lots of fun

physically fit /'fiz e kel le fet/ (adj.) the body's a 10; no room for improvement

rock /'rak/ (n.) 1. appreciates good music; 2. possibly purchased pet rock some years ago

romantic interlude /wen 'nit stand/ (adv.) short but sweet

seeking same /'sek in sam/ (adj.) I'm OK, I'm OK

sensitive /'sen(t) set iv/ (adj.) Ivory Soap user

sensuous /'sench e wes/ (adj.) a good touch

soulmate /'sol mat/ (n.) temperamentally suited

straight /'strat/ (n.) five cards in sequence

successful /sek 'ses fel/ (adj.) will keep you in the style to which you *want* to become accustomed

TLC /'tak te and se/ (n.) tender loving care; will stick to you like cement

together /'weth it/ (n.) one in body and soul with one's self to accomplish oneness

unencumbered /en in 'kem berd/ (adj.) no problems, no relatives, no dependents, no pets, no fun

uninhibited /'en tu 'so pers/ (adj.) a person who will walk nude at the Superbowl

varied interests /'per plekst/ (n.) watches TV less than 10 hours per day

well-proportioned /38-24-36/ (adj.) big melons

7.

PERSONAL STRATEGY

PUBLICATIONS GUIDE

NOTE: Most publications count box numbers and phone numbers as two words; special typesetting usually available for extra charge. Rates, deadline, etc., subject to change by date of book publication; "forwarding fee" is charge to respondents to forward their replies to advertisers on an each-letter basis.

STATE	NAME	CIRCU-LATION	FREQUENCY	RATE	DEADLINE	COMMENTS
Alabama	*Country Companions* 556 Kumquat St. Fairhope, AL 36532		Bimonthly	$7.95/1-50 words; $11.95/ 50-100 words; $15.95/101-150 words; 25¢ each additional word	10th of month preceding issue date	Reduced rate for subscribers
California	*Chico News & Review* 120 W. 2nd St. Chico, CA 95926	24,000	Weekly	$3 for 30 words or less; 10¢ each additional word; no box chg; p/u only	Monday, 5 PM	Regional, northern California. MC, Visa
	BAM 1756 1/2 N. Las Palmas Hollywood, CA 90028	110,000	Semi-monthly	$12.50/1st 15 words and 50¢ each additional word	Every other Friday for publication 14 days later	Regional. Visa, MC. 10% discount on six insert orders

Publication	Circulation	Frequency	Rates	Deadline	Notes
Los Angeles Magazine Classified Bazaar P.O. Box 49999 Los Angeles, CA 90049	162,000	Monthly	$2.35/word; 12-word minimum; $6 box chg.	1st of month preceding issue date	Regional. MC, Visa. Multiple insertion gets discount
LA Weekly 5325 Sunset Blvd. Los Angeles, CA 90027	65,000	Weekly	$5 for 4 lines; each additional line $1.50; 4 line minimum	Friday, 5:30 PM	Regional. MC, Visa
Contact High P.O. Box 500 Mendocino, CA 95460	10,000	Bimonthly	$5/50 words; $10/100 words; special rates for photos	1st of month preceding issue date	National. Subscriber rates less than general rate. Multiple insertion gets discount. $1 forwarding fee
Pacific Sun 21 Corte Madera Ave. Mill Valley, CA 94941	26,000	Weekly	$1/line (30 spaces)	Friday, 4 PM	Regional. SASE gets info and tear sheets

STATE	NAME	CIRCU-LATION	FREQUENCY	RATE	DEADLINE	COMMENTS
	BAM The California Music Mag. 5951 Canning St. Oakland, CA 94609	110,000	Semi-monthly	$12.50/1st 15 words and 50¢ each additional word	Every other Friday for publication 14 days later	Regional. Visa, MC. 10% discount on six insert orders
	Suttertown News 2791 24th St. Sacramento, CA 95818	4,200	Weekly	8¢/word; no box chg.; p/u only	Monday	Regional. Cash in advance
	San Francisco: The Magazine of Northern California 973 Market St. San Francisco, CA 94103	42,000	Monthly	$1.50/word	25th of month 2 months preceding issue date	Regional. MC, Visa. Multiple insertion gets discount
	San Francisco Bay Guardian 2700 19th St. San Francisco, CA 94110	40,000	Weekly	25¢/word; $2.75 extra for bold headline; $4 box chg.	Friday, 2 PM	Regional. MC, Visa

Publication	Circulation	Frequency	Rates	Deadline	Notes
Santa Barbara News & Review 735 State St. Santa Barbara, CA 93101	30,000	Weekly	$4/4 lines; 75¢ each additional line; $2 box chg.; p/u only	Tuesday noon	Regional. MC, Visa. Call in service available
COUPLES . . . The Digest of Human Relations 3420 Ocean Park Blvd. Suite 3000 Santa Monica, CA 90405	400,000	Monthly	$15/18 words; $25/30 words; and so on	4 months preceding issue date	National. MC, Visa. Multiple insertion gets discount. $1 forwarding fee. Personal ads apply to unmarried individuals only
Intro P.O. Box Intro Studio City, CA 91640	100,000	Monthly	$15/1–30 words; $25/31–60 words; on up	45 days prior to cover date	National. Visa. $1 forwarding fee. $2 gets sample copy. Ads placed at editors' discretion and geographically divided

STATE	NAME	CIRCU-LATION	FREQUENCY	RATE	DEADLINE	COMMENTS
Colorado	*Beyond Monogamy* P.O. Box 6877 Denver, CO 80206	1,000	9 times a year	$3/40 words; 5¢ each additional word; coded ads $1 extra	1st of month preceding issue date	National. $9/year subscription rate; must be subscriber to advertise; $1 forwarding fee
	Westword 1610 15th St. Denver, CO 80202	48,000	Biweekly	$4/12 words; 10¢ each additional word; $6 box chg.	Monday, 5 PM preceding publication	Regional. Cash in advance
Connecti-cut	*Connecticut Magazine* P.O. Box 907 Fairfield, CT 06430	60,000	Monthly	$1.20/word; $5 box chg.; $15 minimum	20th of 2d month preceding issue date	Regional. Check or money order. Multiple insertion gets discount
	Hartford Advocate 30 Arbor St. Hartford, CT 06105	90,000	Weekly	30¢/word; $3 minimum; $3 box chg.	Thursday, 3 PM	Regional, Connecticut. MC, Visa

	Circulation	Frequency	Rates	Deadline	Notes
New Haven Advocate 1184 Chapel St. New Haven, CT 06511	75,000	Weekly	20¢/word; $2 box chg.; $3 minimum	3 PM Thursday	Regional. Will forward if advertiser provides SASE. Mail held for only 1 month after ad runs
District of Columbia					
City Paper 919 6th St., N.W. Washington, DC 20001	50,000	Biweekly	first 25 words free; each additional word 25¢; $5 box chg.	Wednesday, one week prior to publication	Regional. Cash in advance
New Republic Magazine 1220 19th St., N.W. Washington, DC 20036	80,000	Weekly	$1/word; $4.50 box number chg.	19 days prior to Wednesday issue date	National. MC, Visa. Will reject ads with copy they find objectionable
Washingtonian Magazine 1828 L St., N.W. Washington, DC 20036	101,000	Monthly	$1.50/word; 15-word minimum; $15 box chg.	1st of the month preceding issue date	Regional. MC, Visa. Responses forwarded for 3 months.

STATE	NAME	CIRCU-LATION	FREQUENCY	RATE	DEADLINE	COMMENTS
Florida	*Miami Magazine* Box 340008 Coral Gables, FL 33134	30,000	Monthly	90¢/word; 15-word minimum; $5 box number/box chg.	20th of the month 2 months preceding date of issue	Regional
	East Coast Singles P.O. Box 83 Palm Beach, FL 33480	20,000	Bimonthly	$10/1–25 words; $16/50 words; and so on	See current issue for info	$1 forwarding fee. Multiple insertion gets discount
	Florida Singles P.O. Box 8383 Palm Beach, FL 33480	11,000	Bimonthly	$12/25 words; $19/50 words; $27/75 words; $35/100 words	See current issue for info	$1 forwarding fee. Multiple insertion gets discount
	Sunshine State Singles Magazine P.O. Box 880 Boynton Beach, FL 33435		Quarterly	50¢/word; $8 minimum	March 1, June 1, September 1, December 1	$1 forwarding fee—use larger envelope for responses; special abbreviations—write for details

Tampa Bay Life 4382 El Prado Box 18768 Tampa, FL 33679	15,500	Monthly	$1/word; 15 word minimum; $5 box number chg.	First Friday of preceding month	Most ads regional; however, 1,200 subscribers out of state. Responses forwarded weekly
Tampa Magazine 4100 W. Kennedy Tampa, FL 33609	18,000	Monthly	$1/word; 15-word minimum; no box chg.	5 weeks before issue date	Regional. MC, Visa
Illinois *The Weekly* 17 E. University Champaign, IL 61820	28,000	Weekly	$2/10 words or less; $3.50/20 words or less; $5.50 per column inch; photo booth personals $10 including wording	Monday, 4 PM	Regional. MC, Visa

STATE	NAME	CIRCU-LATION	FREQUENCY	RATE	DEADLINE	COMMENTS
	One Times One Box 1365 Evanston, IL 60204		every other month	$10 for 25 words or less; 30¢ per word thereafter		$2 forwarding fee for first response; $1 for additional responses; attach first-class postage for forwarding responses—send in larger envelope addressed to magazine
	Illinois Times 610 S. 7th St. P.O. Box 3524 Springfield, IL 62708	20,000	Weekly	30¢ word; $1.50 box chg.	Monday, 5 PM	Regional. MC, Visa. Multiple insertion gets discount
Indiana	*Indianapolis Magazine* 363 N. Illinois Indianapolis, IN 46204	18,000	Monthly	80¢/word	6 weeks preceding issue date	Regional

State	Publication	Circulation	Frequency	Rates	Deadline	Notes
Iowa	*Des Moines Register and Tribune* 715 Locust St. Des Moines, IA 50304	400,000	Weekly	$2.50/line; $12 box chg.	Friday, 5 PM	Regional, Iowa
Maine	*Maine Times* 41 Main St. Topsham, ME 04086	18,000	Weekly	$1.60/line; 2 line minimum; $1.50 box chg. + wording	Monday noon	New England region. Cash in advance
Maryland	*City Paper* 2612 N. Charles St. Baltimore, MD 21218	40,000	Weekly	first 25 words free; each additional word 25¢; $10 box chg.	Friday noon	Regional
Massachusetts	*Boston Magazine* St. James Ave. Boston, MA 02116	110,000	Monthly	$1.50/word; 10 word minimum; p.o. boxes & phone numbers 2 words; $13 box chg.	4th of month preceding issue date	MC, Visa, AE. Multiple insertion gets discount

STATE	NAME	CIRCU-LATION	FREQUENCY	RATE	DEADLINE	COMMENTS
	Boston Phoenix 100 Massachusetts Ave. Boston, MA 02115	134,000	Weekly	3 lines $6.25; each additional line $2.25; $5 box chg.	Wednesday, 5 PM	Regional. MC, Visa, AE. Call in service available
	East/West Journal 17 Station St. P.O. Box 1200 Brookline, MA 02147	65,000	Monthly	60¢/word	5th of month 2 months preceding issue	National. All ads must be typewritten
	Harvard Magazine 7 Ware St. Cambridge, MA 02138	110,000	Bimonthly	$1.50/word; 10-word minimum; $5 box chg.	6 weeks preceding issue date	National. MC, Visa. Multiple insertion gets discount
	Valley Advocate 50 Prospect Hatfield MA 01038	100,000	Weekly	30¢/word; $3 minimum; $3 box chg.	Thursday, 3 PM	Regional, Massachusetts. MC, Visa

State	Publication	Circulation	Frequency	Rates	Deadline	Notes
	Worcester Magazine 22 Front St. Worcester, MA 01614	46,000	Weekly	13¢/word; 20 word minimum; $2 box chg.	Monday noon	Regional. MC, Visa
Michigan	*Flint Voice* 5005 Lapeer Burton, MI 48509	25,000	Biweekly	free	Friday preceding publication	Regional
	Monthly Detroit 1404 Commonwealth Bldg. Detroit, MI 48226	48,000	Monthly	$1/word; 15-word minimum; $7 box number chg.	1st of the month preceding issue date	Regional. MC, Visa
Minnesota	*Twin Cities Reader* 100 N. 7th Minneapolis, MN 55403	100,000	Weekly	20¢/word; $3 box chg.	Monday noon	Regional. MC, Visa
Missouri	*Riverfront Times* 1917 Park Ave. St. Louis, MO 63104	26,000	Weekly	25 words or less, free; $2/ each additional 25 words	Friday noon	Regional, entertainment magazine

STATE	NAME	CIRCU-LATION	FREQUENCY	RATE	DEADLINE	COMMENTS
	St. Louis Magazine 7110 Oakland St. Louis, MO 63117	50,000	Monthly	$1/word; $10 minimum	1st of month preceding issue date	Regional
New Jersey	Ascension from the Ashes 153 George St., Suite 1 New Brunswick, NJ 08901	20,000	Quarterly	50 words free	1/1, 3/1, 6/1, 9/1	National
	New Jersey Monthly 1101 State Rd., Bldg. i Princeton, NJ 08540	95,000	Monthly	$1.50/word; 12-word minimum; $8 box chg.	25th of month 2 months preceding issue date	Regional. Cash, MC, Ads forwarded indefinitely
	Atlantic City Magazine 1637 Atlantic Ave. Atlantic City, NJ 08401	50,000	every other month	$1/word; 10 word minimum; $12 box chg.	5th of month prior to issue date	National. Visa

New York	*Selling Post* 45-38 Bell Blvd. Bayside, NY 11361	72,000	Weekly	ads free when you buy magazine	Thursday noon	Regional
	Mensa Bulletin 1701 W. 3 St., Suite 1R Brooklyn, NY 11223	50,000	Monthly	45¢/word; $3 box number chg.	10 weeks preceding issue date	Must be Mensa member in good standing to advertise
	Ithaca Times P.O. Box 27 Ithaca, NY 14850	16,000	Weekly	25¢/word; 12 word minimum; p/u only	Tuesday noon	Regional
	High Times 17 W. 60 St. New York, NY 10023	300,000		$4/word; 10-word minimum	90 days preceding issue date	National
	Metropolitan Almanac 80 E. 11 St. New York, NY 10003	9,000	Weekly	$1 to $3/line (differs depending on size of type you want); $4 minimum chg.	Thursday noon for the issue 8 days later	Regional. Responses forwarded for 6 weeks after ad appears. 50¢ forwarding fee

147

STATE	NAME	CIRCU-LATION	FREQUENCY	RATE	DEADLINE	COMMENTS
	New York Review of Books 250 W. 57th St. New York, NY 10019	105,000	Weekly	$1/word; 15-word minimum; $7 box chg.	6 weeks preceding issue date	National. Multiple insertion gets discount
	Our Town 1751 Second Ave., #202 New York, NY 10028	111,000	Weekly	$1/word; minimum 15 words; box chg. $6; $2.50 charge for mailing responses to advertiser	Tuesday, 10 AM	Regional. MC, Visa
	Pillow Talk 215 Lexington Ave. New York, NY 10016	85,000	Bimonthly	$5/ad	No specific deadline but ads run about 5 months after submission	National. Deadline for responses is last day of month on cover

Village Voice 842 Broadway New York, NY 10003	150,000	Weekly	$6 pick-up chg.; $8 mail forwarding chg.	Friday 5:30 PM	National. Personal address/phone numbers cannot be used. Box number expires 4 weeks after last appearance of ad. Pick-up only on Tues. and Thurs. between 2 and 5 PM
City Newspaper 250 N. Goodman Rochester, NY 14607	8,000	Weekly	$9/first 15 words; 25¢ each additional word; runs 2 weeks. $2 box chg. for p/u, $5 for mail	Monday noon	Regional. MC, Visa

STATE	NAME	CIRCU-LATION	FREQUENCY	RATE	DEADLINE	COMMENTS
	Syracuse New Times P.O. Box 979 Syracuse, NY 13201	45,000	Weekly	25¢/word; 10 word minimum; $2 box chg.	Friday, 2 PM	Regional. MC, Visa
North Carolina	*Mother Earth News* P.O. Box 70 Hendersonville, NC 28791	1,000,000	Bimonthly	$4/word; $5 all caps; min. insertion $70	7th of month 2 months preceding issue date	National
Ohio	*Cleveland Magazine* 1621 Euclid Ave. Cleveland, OH 44115	60,000	Monthly	$1.30/word; $10 box chg.	1st of month preceding issue date	Regional. MC, Visa
	The Scene 1314 Huron Rd. Cleveland, OH 44115	200,000+	Weekly	35¢/word; 15 word minimum; $4 box chg.	Tuesday noon	Regional. Multiple insertion gets discount. Newspaper is free

	Circulation	Frequency	Rates	Deadline	Notes
Living Single 40 S. Third St. Columbus, OH 43215	10,000	Monthly	one month $10; two months $19; three months $27; for 100 words or less	six weeks preceding issue date	Regional, Cleveland Columbus. $1 forwarding fee; use blank envelope and attach first-class postage for forwarding responses—send in larger envelope directly to magazine
Oregon					
Willamette Valley Observer The Atrium Suite 216 99 W. 10th Eugene, OR 97401	10,000	Weekly	20¢/word; $2 minimum; box chg. $2 for p/u, $3 for mailing; subscribers get 25 words free with coupon	Thursday, 5 PM	Regional. Cash in advance
Solo 1832 N.E. Broadway Portland, OR 97232	2,400	Monthly	50¢/word; $1.50 handling chg.	15th of each month	Regional. Cash, money order. Ads forwarded indefinitely

STATE	NAME	CIRCU-LATION	FREQUENCY	RATE	DEADLINE	COMMENTS
	Willamette Week 320 S.W. Stark Portland, OR 97204	50,000	Weekly	$1/line; $4.50 box chg.	Friday noon	Regional, Oregon. MC, Visa
Pennsyl-vania	*Electricity* 262 S. 12 St. Philadelphia, PA		Weekly	$2/20 words; 10¢ each additional word; $5 box chg.	Fridays 5 PM	Regional Visa, MC; multiple insertion gets discount
	Erie Magazine P.O. Box 7159 Erie, PA 16510	17,000	Bimonthly	$4/line	One month prior to publication	Regional. Cash or money order. No box service
	Germantown Courier 311 E. Lancaster Ave. Philadelphia, PA 19003	28,000	Weekly	$3.75 for 12 words; 15¢ each additional word; $2 box chg.	Monday, 4:30 PM	Regional. Discount of $1 if ad costs $5 or more

		Circulation	Frequency	Rates	Deadline	Coverage
	Philadelphia Magazine 1500 Walnut St. Philadelphia, PA 19102	140,000	Monthly	$2/word; $14.50 box chg.	1st of month preceding issue date	Regional. MC, Visa, American Express. Multiple insertion gets discount. Responses forwarded for 1 year
Texas	*D. Magazine* 1925 Jacinto Dallas, TX 75201	70,000	Monthly	$1.50/word; 15-word minimum; $10 box chg.	25th of month 2 months preceding issue date	Regional. MC
	Houston City 315 W. Alabama Houston, TX 77006	60,000	Monthly	$1.50/word; 15-word minimum; no box chg.	25th of month 2 months preceding issue date	Regional
Vermont	*Vanguard Press* 87 College St. P.O. Box 928 Burlington, VT 05401	25,000	Weekly	25¢/word; $5 minimum; $1.25 box chg.; $3 mail out chg.	Wednesday, 5 PM	Regional, Vermont. MC, Visa

153

STATE	NAME	CIRCU-LATION	FREQUENCY	RATE	DEADLINE	COMMENTS
Washington	*The Weekly* 1932 1st Ave., Suite 605 Seattle, WA 98101	25,000	Weekly	35¢/word; $5 box chg.	Friday noon	Regional. Will reject ads with copy they find objectionable
Wisconsin	*City Lights* 302 E. Washington Ave. Madison, WI 53703	20,000	Biweekly	75¢/line; 3 line minimum; $3 box chg.	Friday preceding publication	Regional. Cash in advance
	Isthmus 636 W. Washington Madison, WI 53703	31,000	Weekly	$1/line; $1 box chg.	Monday, 5 PM	Regional. MC, Visa

Publication	Circulation	Frequency	Rates	Deadline	Notes
The Progressive 409 E. Main St. Madison, WI 53703	40,000	Monthly	60¢/word; 10-word minimum; $2 box chg.	15th of month preceding issue date	National. Check or money order. Multiple insertion gets discount. Appeals to activists, environmentalists
Canada					
Saturday Night 70 Bond St. Suite 500 Toronto, Ontario M5B 2J3 Canada	130,000	Monthly	$1.50/word; $5 box chg.	6 weeks preceding issue date	Multiple insertion gets discount
Toronto Life 59 Front St. E. Toronto, Ontario M5E 1B2 Canada	78,000	Monthly	$1.50/word;	45 days preceding issue date	Regional. MC. Multiple insertion gets discount

ABOUT THE AUTHOR

Female (30), impulsive, "Funny Girl"-type, single and available; nondegreed but can keep up with the best; as aggressive in driving as she is in life; parks in fire lanes; rushes everywhere and never stands in line; must always have first-row seats; predictably unpretentious; dabbles in spa sociality; a true friend, generous to the point of being extravagant; a real entertainer with a creative streak that matches few (an asset to any party); not totally eccentric and not as obnoxious as she sounds.

1 0 -10